WHEN WOMEN LEAD

Or, Some of the Myriad Reasons Why

Many Women In Leadership
=
A Better World

Shirley M Osborne

WHEN WOMEN LEAD

*My satisfaction comes from
my commitment to advancing a better world.*
- Faye Wattleton

2

i want to apologize to all the women

i have called pretty.

before i've called them intelligent or brave.

-    Rupi Kaur

WHEN WOMEN LEAD

PREFACE

Like many millions of people around the world, I have social media accounts. I use them for work and for other stuff. From time to time, I post memes, by which I mean that I superimpose some words onto a picture and post it somewhere in the cybersphere.

I did that with the first wave of promotions for this book. Just as the book was nearing completion, I posted a series of six pictures of famous women's faces. Across the lower half of each picture I had written "WOMEN IN LEADERSHIP =" followed by one of several phrases such as, for example, SAFER COUNTRIES, HEALTHIER PEOPLE, GREATER FREEDOM, A BETTER WORLD.

When I saw that one woman had demanded to know, "Any woman?" my hackles shot up and immediately, I shot back, "Many women!!" I had heard that kind of dismissal of women's leadership so many times in my life! Too many times. Even from women! From too many women.

"Yeah, but…not just *any* woman," they say.

"We have to be careful to pick the *right* woman," they specify.

Then, almost immediately after I clicked POST to respond to this woman, I dissolved into laughter. "Yes! Yes. Yes!!" I said out loud to the universe – and my cat. "Yes, Girrrl!" I said to that sister. "Thank you. Many women! Many, MANY women. Not *any* woman. Not *more* women. Many women!"
It was a lightbulb moment for me. And the title of this book was written:

Some of the myriad reasons why

MANY WOMEN IN LEADERSHIP

=

A BETTER WORLD

We've all seen at one time or another, that one short string of words change the dynamics in a room, shut women down, push women out of consideration, time after time restrict the probabilities of women's lives – individually and in the collective. We have seen, far too often, how these little sentences, voicing this ostensibly very reasonable concern, are so blithely and so routinely deployed to force women in general out of the runnings, force individual women into the position of having to prove the mettle, the capabilities, the very worth, even the basic human goodness of all women before even one woman might be permitted to enter or to ascend. The effect of that one phrase in the regard always of just one woman, is that women as a group are restricted, ignored, kept out and held back.

That does not work for me. That does not work for women. It does not work for men!!

It does not serve the world.

Yes. There have been, there are now and there will be women who function in the old, unhelpful paradigms. There will be those women who will hurt more than they help, who will work against every positive thing written about in this book. Those will be the "any" women, the ones who sometimes bring even me to wish we could be particular and ultra-discerning and ultra-selective and just wait for the "right" women before we pick any one. But we cannot do that. We cannot wait. We must do the best we can with what we have. And we must do it now.

We must play against the odds – or with the odds or to beat the odds or whatever proves useful. We just must play. We will win some and we shall certainly lose some, but if we have many women vying for positions then we will certainly get many women into positions of leadership, not just the odd one here and there. And the odds are, we shall win much more than we lose – all of us, men included, and across all aspects, sectors and possibilities.

In writing this book, I have looked back into history and relied on contemporary occurrences to find evidence to support my thesis. *"There are, of course,"* the literature reminded me, *"notable exceptions to the idea that female leaders are more compassionate, nurturing or nonviolent leaders."*

I get that. I acknowledge and accept that. Clearly, I'm not claiming any perfection for women. I'm not even asking that we strive for that. I am asserting that better is possible for our world – much, much better – and that we will get to better, rise to better to the extent that we are led ALSO by women. By many women.

Shirley Osborne

Providence, Montserrat

Phoenix, Arizona

WHEN WOMEN LEAD

WHEN WOMEN LEAD

10

CLARIFICATIONS

Leadership should be born out of the understanding of the needs of those who would be affected by it.
- Marian Anderson

I believe we should begin by making it very clear, above all, that "women in leadership" is not an "either…or…" proposition.

Contrary to what many people prefer to believe, there is absolutely no truth whatsoever to the rumour that women want to "take over the world" so as to disenfranchise men, "emasculate" men, or "rule" men. Despite the fears expressed by men in this regard, women in general really have no interest in returning upon men these injustices that men have done to women across these many millennia.

To put the very finest point on this, it is not the case that women want that "women in leadership" be an "*either* men *or* women" situation. It is, rather, that women want that the leadership of our world be balanced, comprise "*both* men *and* women" for the good of both men and women. Most women and many men know that it would be a good thing. A very good thing, indeed. For all and sundry.

It is possibly the case that men experience fear about women in leadership only because…well…only because they do, in fact, deep down, recognise the imbalance, injustice and illogic of the past and current state, and dread a reprisal. In fact, some people suspect that men have these fears because, having taught themselves, for millennia, that it is the right and duty of men to exercise power and control over others, to dominate and disenfranchise, to command others, to annihilate opposition, to see all others as threats and to eliminate all threats, real and perceived, they now truly fear being made to swallow a mouthful of their own medicine. They know that women, too, have been taught that the way of leadership is command and control, dominate or annihilate.

That attitude is now very deeply-ingrained and the lessons of unlearning seem to come with a very steep learning curve – which really ought not be the case given the superior intellect claimed by men!

But women do not want to do that. Women in leadership reject that. For women, leadership is a "both…and…" situation. It is "BOTH men AND women". It is absolutely a matter of "…and *women.*"

Writing for the World Economic Forum in March 2020, Leanne Kemp says, "Ultimately, the problems we face are not technological, but human – the human system is broken." Women in leadership do not want to replace men in that broken system. Women want to work alongside men, in partnership, to build a better system. Women want both groups of human beings contributing the highest and best of themselves so as to improve, generate, create, arrive at the system that works the very best for men, women, children, community, industry, government, the planet, the cosmos, the universe – in short, for everyone and everything.

Men have been the rulers of the universe for a very long time now and during that time, much that is good and helpful has been brought to the entirety of humankind. It has not been brought only by men. Women have played very significant parts. The problem is that women's contributions have been largely unacknowledged. In many instances now on the record, men have stolen the credit, denying, in as many words, any woman's capacity for high accomplishment. In the sciences, there has been a pattern in which the accomplishments of female scientists have historically been under-recognized, and credit disproportionately given to their male colleagues. Science historian Margaret Rossiter, termed this the "Matilda effect".

While working as a research associate at the King's College London in the biophysics unit in 1951, Rosalind Franklin and her student Raymond Gosling discovered that there were two forms of DNA. Competing scientists James Watson and Francis Crick used Franklin's findings as a basis for their DNA model and won a Nobel Prize for it in 1962.

Experimental physicist Chien-Shiung Wu, conducted a series of experiments that disproved the Law of Parity. Two other researchers, Tsung-Dao Lee and Chen-Ning Yang, had already theorized the invalidity of the Law, but they needed the evidence that Wu had acquired. In 1954, Lee and Yang were awarded the Nobel Prize in Physics. Wu was not recognised.

As recently as 2017, Lara Rutherford-Morrison reported that, "When Hungarian swimmer Katinka Hosszu, won gold in the Rio Olympics this summer, a commentator identified her coach and husband as "the guy responsible for turning [her] into a whole different swimmer."

Contribution – and especially leadership – by women has been so deliberately, relentlessly and ruthlessly prohibited, and then discounted and denied where it did still somehow manage to occur, that it is matter for much marvel, indeed, that women still are capable of any competence.

The systems enacted by men have denied both women's leadership and women's agency. Women wholeheartedly acknowledge the natural abilities and honed skills of men, and believe that there is a relationship of equivalence in diversity between those and the skills and abilities of women. Women want that equivalence recognised. The entire discourse around women in leadership rests, logically, upon the foundations of gender equality – equality of access and opportunity – and the acceptance that human society is enhanced by the diversity that women represent.

Diversity is an important consideration in human relations for the simple fact that women and men are, by nature, as diverse as we are similarly human. Diversity is a characteristic of Nature. Diverse is not a synonym for unequal. Diversity is natural and desirable, and it is very necessary. It is as natural, necessary and desirable amongst the members within any group as it is between and amongst different groups. Men and women are different and that is good. Men and women are not unequal and that is good.

Yet, all our societies and communities have had to struggle with this burden of inequality for millennia. The motivations and the evolution of this imposition are the story of the human race. It is the story of oppression and tyranny, of uneven progress, of denial and failure – of stymied advancement and rejected opportunity, and of survival in spite of oppression and tyranny, despite unrealised potential. One can hardly imagine what might have been the state of advancement of humanity at this point, had this burden been lifted long ago, or better yet, not allowed to take shape, in the first place.

The human race has survived largely because women-in-general have endured, have subordinated their individual ambitions and desires to the continuation of the human race. Women have subsisted, and have continued to procreate, in that lowly state. Women have survived by renouncing merit, suppressing their humanness and subjugating the instinct for – and the right to – sovereignty. These are they who have kept the human race propagating – and safe from extinction.

There have been women who chose to die rather than live as chattel and non-entity owned, bought and sold by men; women who took to the hills, literally and figuratively, to escape control and subjugation by men; women who sent their babies into the afterlife to save them the horrors of enslavement and dehumanisation; women who fought to the death for autonomy and personhood; women who railed against the system. And these are they who have kept alive the truth of the humanness and sovereignty of women, with all its attendant rights – and the dignity and potentiality of the human species, with all its faults and failings.

And so it is that, jointly, these two groups of women have enabled the human race to survive millennia of trial and error, hardship and terror, and success and failure. Jointly, these two groups of women have ensured that the human race has managed to survive to achieve the progress we have, to arrive at today, at this latest possible inflection point – this, the year two thousand and twenty of the Common Era – a year that has brought us a pandemic that is truly worldwide, economic troubles that have affected every country, and social upheaval that is global in its reach.

This 2020, which seems an entire era all by itself, could be another truly pivotal and transformational moment for the entire human race. This could be a moment when the one proverbial drop causes the cup to overflow. It could be one of those moments when that one last straw actually does break the camel's back.

Recent decades of simmering tensions and festering resistance – neo-colonialism, trade wars, racism, puritanical religious fundamentalism, political oppression, mass migration, and such – brought to a head by information technology, murder in the streets and a new, deadly virus, could bestow upon the year 2020, historical significance akin to that of 1914, perhaps, and certainly greater than 1968's, say. It could. It could, but it might not. In any case, whatever the peoples of the world might make – or fail to make – of this opportunity, 2020 has already earned the distinction of being a seminal moment in the history of the world – it has caused thought and reflection. Whether that will amount to any more valuable action is left to be seen, but its potential for lasting significance has, largely, been recognised.

Thinking people have known that we would at some point come to a time like this, arrive at what could be critical mass, a moment in which we could shift the paradigm once again, if we dared. They have known that cause matters, so that an opening brought about by a breakdown, a space opened up by the destruction of something, presents an opportunity for rebuilding that is limited only by the quality of the leadership which ultimately takes it on.

So, could the women leaders who have been managing in these extraordinary times and world-changing occurrences with such unparalleled – and undeniable – skill and facility, finally demolish the boundaries to general acceptance of leadership by women? Could this be the moment when women leaders come to be taken as seriously as men, and in which women in leadership finally becomes the norm? Could this truly be a critical mass moment that finally reformats and improves the unbalanced and unstable systems of our world? Could this be the moment when women leaders finally come into their own?

"Women's ability to make an impact in male-dominated institutions will be limited, until they are represented in numbers large enough to have a collective voice, until they reach a 'critical mass'," writes Elizabeth Powley for UNICEF. She was reporting specifically on *The Impact of Women Legislators on Policy Outcomes Affecting Children and Families in Postgenocide Rwanda*, but the principle holds in every other country, scenario and circumstance.

Forbes magazine says that Sally Helgesen is the world's premier expert on women's leadership. Writing in Strategy+Business in July 2020, Helgesen posits that, "The [COVID19] pandemic is disrupting organizations, economies, and societies around the world, forcing many of us to alter how we live, work, communicate, and think about a future that appears more uncertain than we had previously imagined. As we move through the crisis, the jarring impact of this shift will inevitably reshape what people will look for in their leaders — which should have far-reaching consequences for women."

Those "far-reaching consequences" could include a final, definitive shift in popular perceptions of women in leadership in some parts of the world, which will, undoubtedly, energise and accelerate the march in the rest.

Helgesen also says, "First, highly visible female leaders such as Angela Merkel of Germany, Tsai Ing-Wen of Taiwan, Jacinda Ardern of New Zealand, and Mette Frederiksen of Denmark have offered strong examples of leadership during crisis, as have Governor Gretchen Whitmer of Michigan and Mayor Lori Lightfoot of Chicago...The big takeaway is that although surveys have for more than a decade shown that people in general, view women as more trustworthy than men, men have continued to rank higher on having the strength to lead in times of crisis. But what we are now witnessing suggests that this perception may be about to shift."

In April 2020, Forbes magazine published a contribution written by Avivah Wittenberg-Cox which, in its title, asked and answered a burning question, *"What Do Countries With The Best Coronavirus Responses Have In Common? Women Leaders."* In that article she says, "Generally, the empathy and care which all of these female leaders have communicated seems to come from an alternate universe than the one we have gotten used to. It's like their arms are coming out of their videos to hold you close in a heart-felt and loving embrace. Who knew leaders could sound like this? Now we do."

In September, she followed that up in with, *Women Leaders' Competence On COVID: The Proof*. In this second article, Wittenberg-Cox cites the findings of academic research undertaken by Supriya Garikipati and Uma Kambhampati, of Liverpool and Reading Universities respectively, in the UK, which "confirms that COVID-19 outcomes are better in female-led countries."

Garikipati and Kambhampati say that in their research, they matched female-led countries against those with male leaders based on COVID-relevant social and demographic variables and their data showed clearly that "it is, in fact, **leadership** that drives differences in initial COVID outcomes."

Of course, leadership is a factor in every sector of human living at all times, crisis or no crisis. In fact, good leadership helps to prevent crisis. Every group that gathers, every organization that forms, appoints a leader, formally or tacitly, regardless of its size or functions – a group of small boys at play, a women's book club, a family, a company, a country. Somebody once said somewhere that "a leaderless organization is merely a muddle of men and machine; a country without leadership is anarchy; a society without leadership is a violent and dangerous place to live."

The old, outdated tropes about leadership are being challenged and displaced, however, eroded day by day by new knowledge and new thinking – and by the entry of women into the highest chairs of leadership. The idea of the "supreme male ruler" whose every desire is diktat is disappearing. "Domination and control" is fast losing its legitimacy and force. Empathy, cooperation and a different quality of communication are making the difference.

In the Journal of Public Health Management and Practice, in 2015, Moran and Beitsch write, "Leaders help themselves and others do the right things. They set direction, craft an inspiring vision, and…guide their organization…to the right destination in a smooth and efficient way."

Many decades before that, Chester Barnard had defined leadership as "the ability of a superior to influence the behaviour of a subordinate or group and persuade them to follow a particular course of action." Persuade, not force.

Influence and persuasion constitute leadership of a very particular quality, a more subtle, and ultimately a more powerful, sustainable and enduring kind than that acquired through force or violence. Influence is unforced and un-forceable. The most powerful kind of leadership is, also, unforced. People lead and people follow, for good and for evil; they follow if they are forced to, until something more forceful shows up, and they follow if they want to.

The most powerful and effective leadership, logically, occurs when people want to be led. They will allow themselves to be led by a particular leader, because they want to move in a particular direction, and they will resist the leadership should any part of that change.

With very few exceptions, the bulk of histories however recorded or transmitted, recount the accomplishments and leadership exploits of men, specifically and almost exclusively, and sometimes provide the evidence of women being denied opportunity to achieve. In his first letter to Timothy, St. Paul of the early Christian church wrote, "I do not permit a woman to teach or to assume authority over a man; she must be quiet." History is replete with some very unpleasant examples of what happens when only men are allowed to assume authority, and the ever-growing mountain of evidence of violence and the historical abuse of authority in the Roman Catholic church, makes it one prime, and deeply unfortunate, example.

The history of violence specifically perpetrated against women and that is today being referred to as the war against women, has been the focus of much scholarly and journalistic examination. In her book, *The War Against Women,* Marilyn French posits that perhaps men's need to dominate women may be based in men's own sense of marginality or emptiness resulting from a decrease in dependence on hunting in ancient societies and the consequent reduction in power and social prestige which being hunter had previously conferred.

The three hundred years of witch hunting in Europe and America, for example, the burning, drowning and other forms of torture and killing, overwhelmingly directed at women, are partly explained by economic and demographic changes, writes Nachman Ben-Yehuda in an American Journal of Sociology article entitled *The European Witch Craze of the 14th to 17th Centuries: A Sociologist's Perspective* while, in the Journal of Social History, Edward Bever, suggests that witch-like behaviours were women's protective responses to the hostility and violence which figured prominently in early modern village and small-town life.

Much of human history is a tale of violence begetting violence, and that thread remains, says Eoin O'Carroll in the Christian Science Monitor. "Humans are very extreme in the direction of the frequency of killing and intergroup aggression," writes primatologist Professor Richard Wrangham, author of *The Goodness Paradox: The Strange Relationship Between Virtue and Violence in Human Evolution.* That aspect of "intergroup aggression" that has so universally and systematically been directed at women has deprived mankind of inestimable contributions that could be made by women for the good and advancement of all.

Women have, indeed, been subject to enforced silence and invisibility, and women's leadership in the many and various fields has often either been claimed by men or not recorded at all, and the offensively productive woman herself dismissed as an aberration, an abnormality. Along the way to male supremacy and the patriarchy, women became the competition and men's fears that women might unseat them, or prove themselves superior or even equal, in anyway, had to have been reduced, therefore – the old dominate and/or annihilate approach. Any occurrences or trends that ever so vaguely appeared a challenge to the authority of men as a group, had to be put down. Again, Edward Bever: the intervention of the state in the form of widespread and protracted witch prosecutions helped change the perceived "nature" of women from the Medieval notion that they were particularly violent and lustful to the modern image of women as gentle and asexual – the opposite of men, in other words, since those characteristics remained accepted, even encouraged and aspirational, for the "real" man.

The 1784 Robert Burns' poem *Man Was Made To Mourn: A Dirge,* includes the oft-cited,

> *Man's inhumanity to man*

> *Makes countless thousands mourn!*

And "man" here would not have been intended to include women because at that time, the term man meant just that, the males of the species. In that era, men were considered the only humans, really; the only beings capable of any deeds worthy of notice. Women were something else entirely; were simply not a consideration at these levels. Violence perpetrated against women – or enslaved persons – was a matter accorded not very much attention at all.

Steven Pinker, the Johnstone Family Professor in the Department of Psychology at Harvard University, has written that, "Cruelty as entertainment, human sacrifice to indulge superstition, slavery as a labour-saving device, conquest as the mission statement of government, genocide as a means of acquiring real estate, torture and mutilation as routine punishment, the death penalty for misdemeanours and differences of opinion, assassination as the mechanism of political succession, rape as the spoils of war, pogroms as outlets for frustration, homicide as the major form of conflict resolution—all were unexceptionable features of life for most of human history." And were the malfeasance, almost entirely, of men.

For the entirety of that "most of human history" timeframe, societies and countries were led by men. That poem cited above, written in the eighteenth century by Robert Burns, also included the verse,

If I'm design'd yon lordling's slave,

By Nature's law design'd,

Why was an independent wish

E'er planted in my mind?

At the time the poem was written, the lives of women in Scotland, as in all of Western Europe – and with very few exceptions, the entire rest of the world – were hardly more autonomous than those of enslaved people, circumscribed as they were by a daughter's duties to her father, a wife's duties to her husband and by the key virtues of chastity and obedience. But Burns was not speaking of the yearnings of any women for agency and autonomy, nor were many other poets and writers of the times.

In *The Journal of Thought,* John Crawford reminds us of "the most common attitude toward women espoused by the masses in eighteenth-century England", by recounting a conversation between Dr. Johnson and Mrs. Knowles in which she is complaining that men have more liberty than women, to which he replies that men labour and suffer danger for women.

When she argues that she still cannot see why men are allowed more indulgences than women and that it gives a superiority to men to which she does not see how they are entitled, Johnson caustically replies, "It is plain, madam, one or the other must have the superiority."

The times have changed and yet, today, Still, today, in the twenty-first century, the vast majority of men regard home-making, childbearing and caretaking to be women's ordained roles and, therefore, not worthy of much serious acknowledgment, even while they continue to enact laws intended to reinforce this status quo and keep women in the subjugate position. It is still true that women are generally not considered capable of contributing to human development to the degree that men are – even within some of the most advanced societies and among the most feminist of men.

Susan M. Cruea wrote that in the 1800s, that, "women were the continual victims of social and economic discrimination. Upper- and middle-class women's choices were limited to marriage and motherhood, or spinsterhood. Both choices resulted in domestic dependency. While they could find jobs as shop girls or factory workers, women were discouraged from being wage earners by the belief that women who earned wages were "unnatural.""

In 2014, Nigerian novelist, Chimamanda Ngozie Adichie recounted, in a now very famous book-length essay and TED talk, that "I remember that as I argued and argued, Okuloma looked at me and said, "You know, you're a feminist." It was not a compliment. I could tell from his tone, the same tone that you would use to say something like, "You're a supporter of terrorism.""

Today, the ignoring and excluding of women continues in varying degrees in every part of the world. Today, the violence against women, violence in many forms that is often deployed specifically to deny women access to positions of leadership, is a constant in every part of the world. In some places, women are trashed and demonized in the media. In some places, they are raped and murdered.

But, recently, Professor Pinker of Harvard University has sought to reassure us about the human race in general, and perhaps, about men in particular. "Conventional history has long shown," he wrote, "that, in many ways, we have been getting kinder and gentler."

Further reassurance can be taken from a study reported in 2016 by José María Gómez, of the

University of Granada in Spain. Looking back across 50,000 years of history from the Paleolithic period to today, it appears to him that these times in which we now live, are our safest times ever, and that today's state society is the safest place ever, for humans – which presumably includes women since women are slowly but surely coming to be considered part of the human race these days, though still a less valuable part and less capable as leaders.

This, too, is changing, slowly, very slowly, but inexorably.

Professor Gomez also says that, "The main message of the study, from our point of view, is that no matter how violent or pacific we are in the origin, we can modulate the level of interpersonal violence by changing our social environment. We can build a more pacific society if we wish." This book submits that ensuring the placement of many women in positions of leadership will contribute, without a doubt, to changing our social environment into a more pacific one.

The advancement towards the more pacific social environment of which Professor Gomez and his colleagues speak, is bolstered, in part, by the smaller-scale developments and advances occurring every day, seemingly insignificant events that together, however, are building a wave. Little drops of water do an ocean make! Without delving too far back into the darkness of human history once again, one of those developments would be, for instance, the year 1919 when a woman first took a seat in the House of Commons, in then Great Britain.

Men who have served in the British Parliament have acknowledged that the mere presence of women in that chamber has made of that ancient bastion of male privilege and bombast, a much brighter and rather gentler place. They put that down to factors such as women's mode of communication and women's preference for *"cooperation and compromise."* One member, evidently willing but obviously still struggling, explained that, "Women wear colour to the Chamber and that does make the place seem altogether more cheerful; less dark and dour. And I think that's even helped to make the male members perhaps somewhat less, uhm, pugnacious…yes! Less pugnacious, I'd say."

On the History of Government site at gov.uk, Dr. Ben Griffin writes in *Thatcher and The Glass Ceiling* that, "Jim Prior, one of the leading figures in Thatcher's first ministry, found it particularly difficult to raise his voice to a woman and engage in the argumentative style which Thatcher encouraged: such behaviour was not gentlemanly. He found her confrontational manner very difficult to stomach.

Another piece of evidence would be Nelson Mandela's victory in South Africa and his very public and oft-restated commitment to women. On World Women's Day in 1996, he said, "As long as women…are looked down upon…As long as outmoded ways of thinking prevent women from making a meaningful contribution to society, progress will be slow."

Another of these moments could be 2012, when the court in Bombay, India, finally made it perfectly legal for a woman to retain her original surname after marriage. "The law is clear now," reports the Times of India, in a country in which women were traditionally completely renamed upon marriage. "A woman is not obliged to take her husband's name after marriage."

Yet another drop in the ocean could have been the year 2018, when women in Saudi Arabia were first allowed their right to drive a vehicle. Amnesty International said that lifting the ban that prohibited women from driving was "a small step in the right direction." "We are ready, and it will totally change our life," said Samira al-Ghamdi, a 47-year-old psychologist from Jeddah, one of the first women to be issued a driver's license.

Over time, these kinds of occurrences and swings have been causing ripples and waves, ripples and waves that build upon each other and that, when the timing and circumstances are right, must certainly combine with larger scale phenomena and become a mighty wave that finally washes away the debris of old, worn-out structures that no longer serve humanity – if ever they did! This mighty wave will leave in its wake a clean slate, a blank page upon which we will write the next chapter, of a higher stage of human development and progress.

In this moment, as I am writing, in 2020, the world is experiencing just such a build-up. If we handle it right, if we are intentional and judicious, we just might arrive at accomplishment and advance rather than aftermath. Will these most recent small and large events – including the global #MeToo movement, the Women's March following the election of Donald Trump to the United States presidency, the COVID-19 pandemic, the skill of women leaders in managing the series of resultant crises, popular response to the police killings of George Floyd and Breonna Taylor, the international and intersecting explosion of Black Lives Matter and the nomination of Kamala Harris to the US vice-presidency – be addition enough to the centuries of struggle to bring about the decisive heave that finally transforms the world in general and women's lives, more particularly?

What is new, exciting and encouraging is that the definition of "leadership" has been expanding recently and is slowly, but very surely, including women and the particular strengths and characteristics that women possess. That is a good thing. A very good thing. For everyone.

It is evident nowadays and being generally acknowledged, that leadership is in constant operation at all levels of human activity and interaction, whether the structure is hierarchical or horizontal, professional or personal – on the lowest rungs as much as at the highest, people lead and are simultaneously being, themselves, led. Leadership is fluid; we are each sometimes leaders, in other roles, we follow. This is a very helpful development for women.

In the early years of women's entry into the corporate world, the expectation among women and the organizations within which they were employed, seemed to be that women would simply slot themselves into the cultures and structures they met, although those had been designed entirely by and for men. As a result, write researchers, it was commonly assumed that any woman who aspired to a high position would need to adopt traditional male behaviours and styles. That is still very much the expectation in some places, but a lot of change has also come to the realm since those awkward and uncomfortable early days. The times – and the expectations – they are a-changin'.

This book is making the argument that women in leadership is, very simply, a good thing; that having many and varied women in leadership in the many and various sectors of human living will lead us to a better world. That is premise and firm conviction resting on solid evidence. The evidence is there. The evidence is overwhelming. The evidence cannot be ignored. The body of evidence is so large that it would be absolutely impossible to contain it in any book of any number of volumes, but even the limited amount contained here is far more than it should take to convince even the man – or woman! – most deeply opposed to women's leadership, on any grounds.

There is more than enough evidence to prove that systems that oppress women are systems that deprive communities and societies of important and necessary contributions, and that these systems deny accomplishment and advancement also to men. There is more than enough evidence to justify and substantiate the unqualified rejection of all of those systems, everywhere.

The world has been changing, and in 2020, more and more people are beginning to understand that a system in which any one group insists on supremacy, domination and oppression of another is fundamentally unjust, profoundly dysfunctional and woefully wasteful.

In 1792, Mary Wollstonecraft wrote, in *Vindication of the Rights of Woman*, that she "does not wish for women to have power over men, but over themselves," and that, "It is justice, not charity, that is wanting in the world." Justice means recognition of the equality of women. Justice means equal access, for women, to resources and opportunities.

Women want, simply, to participate and contribute to the general good without let or hindrance. Women want, simply, to not be obstructed in either the development or the exercise of our capabilities and competencies. Women want, simply, that it be universally accepted that human rights are also women's rights. Women want our rights; nothing more, nothing less.

If leadership is a right, it is also women's.

If leadership is a skill, women must be free to acquire and use it.

If leadership is a duty, it is one that women also can fulfil.

Indeed, women have proven time and time again, through all "the ages of man", that we are, in fact, capable and competent, and certainly smart enough, strong enough and good enough to be leaders in our communities and societies. That is no longer in question.

To continue to deprive humanity of the benefits of women's leadership is to deny humanity its right to evolution and progress.

35

WOMEN IN LEADERSHIP
=
VALUE ADDED

You need not apologize for
being brilliant, talented, gorgeous, rich, or smart.
- Marianne Williamson

There is a "woman" whom scientists have named "mitochondrial Eve". She is the mother of us all, they say. The mother of all mothers.

"She was not the first human," writes Joshua Rapp Learn in the Smithsonian Magazine, but as incredible as it seems, "every other female lineage eventually had no female offspring and so failed to pass on their mitochondrial DNA." Except hers!

"As a result," he asserts, "all humans today can trace their mitochondrial DNA back to this one specific woman. Within her DNA and that of her peers, existed almost all the genetic variation we see in contemporary humans." More than seven and a half billion individuals are currently alive.

In reality, he also writes, a mitochondrial Eve is not the first female of a species, but merely the most *recent* female historically, from which all living animals of a species can trace their ancestry. So, "If you reach deep enough into the past, you always find a common ancestor of everybody," says Marek Kimmel, a professor of statistical genetics and molecular evolution at Rice University, who published a study in 2010 that places the mitochondrial Eve of humans back to around 100,000 to 250,000 years ago. She lived in southern Africa.

In June 2017, National Geographic published an article written by Michael Greshko in which he investigates the evidence that the human race has been around for as many as three hundred thousand years! That evidence was found in a site in Morocco known as Jebel Irhoud. "The residents of this site were not quite the *Homo sapiens* of today," wrote Greshko, "but their teeth closely resemble those in the mouths of modern humans—and their faces looked just like ours."

"The face is the face of somebody you could cross in the metro," says Jean-Jacques Hublin, the paleoanthropologist at the Max Planck Institute for

Evolutionary Anthropology who led the new research. "It's pretty amazing."

Of course, the human species has been able to survive these many hundreds of thousands of years to be in existence still up to today, because the act of procreation is a shared activity; it relies as much on women as on men. This has not always been clear or acknowledged. It is an argument begun in ancient times, that has continued up to this day – whether investment and involvement in the continuation of the species are greater for men or for women. Some assert, with good reason, that women's involvement in child-bearing is many times greater than that of men.

A particularly curious version of the old "the chicken and the pig" ham-and-eggs parable! In the matter of procreation, the men are involved to the extent that chickens are in the production of eggs, but the women are fully, life-changingly committed. In the simplest terms, whereas procreation takes up but a few moments of men's life, it fully uses up many months and then years at a time of women's lives – a little detail that has, anyhow, not prevented men from asserting full and sole ownership of the process and its outcomes!

Aristotle, considered one of humanity's greatest philosophers and thinkers, very clearly stated his belief that women were inferior to men. In his very deeply-studied treatise, Politics, he states, "as regards the sexes, the male is by nature superior and the female inferior, the male, ruler and the female, subject." In his theory of inheritance, he asserted that the human mother provides only a passive material element to the creation of a child, while the father provides the active, "ensouling" element.

In *The Oxford Handbook of Childhood and Education in the Classical World*, Véronique Dasen published *Becoming Human: From the Embryo to the New-born Child*. She asserts that for Aristotle, only the male seed possesses a creative principle. He wrote, she notes, that "the male seed breathes life into the menstrual blood thanks to the generative heat of the pneuma providing form (eidos) to passive (pathetikon) female matter. Menstrual blood is less perfectly concocted than the male seed, he believed, and it contributes only nutritive soul to the child. In this respect, the woman is only a receptacle. All she does, according to him, is provide the space within which the child develops. She is only the oven in which the bun is baked!

For the Hippocratics, Dasen also writes, it was a less unequal concept. They believed that the man and woman each produce a seed (gonos) that is both male and female, and these seeds "mix" together in the uterus, the more vigorous of the two determining the main characteristics of the child, such as sex and physical resemblance. This thinking is yet another instance of men's denying women's contributions to humanity, and it has not entirely been swept away by modern science.

There still remain great swathes of the world, even today, where women are still considered to be not quite fully human, and as such, having no right to many of the generally-accepted "human" rights, notwithstanding the considerable advances in science and technology, and the vast increase in both general knowledge and specialist information.

Even today, the general confoundment about, and resistance to, women's capabilities and capacities, rights, agency and sovereignty persists, perhaps somewhat less intensely in some countries than it had in some earlier eras of recorded human history, but it does persist, and its effects are suffered by the entirety of the human community.

Without needing to go too far back into time or dig too strenuously, we easily find some explanations for the persistence of these noxious notions in the societies of the world. In the Middle East, they are cultured on the teachings of the Abrahamic religions and in the West on these same, as much as on the philosophies of the Ancient Greeks. In Asia, the Hindus and Buddhists are no less misogynistic and misanthropic. Neither are the vast majority of indigenous or local spiritual pathways in anywhere in the world.

Speaking in the US on a Public Broadcasting Service programme about the roles of women in the Christian church, Elizabeth Clark, the John Carlisle Kilgo Professor of Religion and Director of the Graduate Program in Religion at Duke University said, "What seems to happen within the first few centuries is that, whatever limited activities women might have had in the beginning, begin to get curtailed as you have the development of a hierarchy of clergy members with bishops, presbyters and deacons, and it's pretty firmly established that women should not be either bishops or priests. Many church fathers write about this. So that women tend to get excluded from those functions, [though] they do have some roles, [such] as, in the fourth century, joining a group called the widows or deaconesses."

Other religions and traditional social systems in the world are no less repressive of women than the Christians have been, and in many of their sects and offshoots, continue even today to be. In many so-called developing countries, in many Islamic communities, and in many urban enclaves and rural areas in some ostensibly well-developed countries, the status of women can be described as being at a stage of modernity and enlightenment that is two centuries or more behind some others of the societies of the world.

In these countries, the restrictions on and repression of women are so absolute as to make it almost impossible for women to even be able to begin to engage any meaningful struggle – or even conversation – for their sovereignty and personhood. The social, economic, cultural and religious pressures and restrictions are simply too great.

Christian Amanpour, celebrated journalist and international correspondent with CNN, has discussed the astonishment she experienced, despite her deep journalistic expertise, upon discussing love and happiness with a group of Afghan women refugees in Berlin, Germany. Her programme shows her interpreter, another woman, warning her, "We have to be careful with this question. It is a dangerous question." The question she asked a young Afghan woman? "Were you ever told that you also have a right to be loved, to be happy?"

In Hinduism, women still are too often seen as dependent minors who are owned, and need to be controlled by, men. Within Hinduism and under the practice of Hinduism, girls are of little relative value and women are subservient to men in everyday life. This is very clearly demonstrated historically in the traditions surrounding the naming of girl children and the ancient ritual of Sati, though that has now been outlawed. In sati, a woman who outlived her husband was required to kill herself as a sacrifice, by burning herself on her husband's funeral pyre, for without her husband, she was no longer of any value to the community.

Femicide continues to be a terrible scourge in some communities. More than 600 000 girls (aged 0-6 years) are estimated to be missing in India every year, most of them aborted, others are killed, abandoned or neglected to death, all simply because they are girls. Of those girl children who are born, many are given names that mean "unwanted" and despite changes in legislation, child marriage and the dowry system continue. Girls are often renamed completely by the family of the husband when they marry, indicating the transference of ownership from one man, the father to another, the husband. In 2011, a group of just over 250 Indian girls whose Marathi name meant "unwanted", were given a fresh start at a mass renaming ceremony in Maharashtra state – they were allowed to choose new names and legally rename themselves.

However, reports *The Hindu,* in a region where gender bias only starts with the name, and the parents think of daughters as a burden, there is a possibility that the change will only be restricted to the renaming ritual, and not reflect in the actual change in mindset. Satara District Health Officer Dr. Bhagwan Pawar, told *The Hindu* that the renaming will send out a positive message to people, that girls must be welcomed in the family. "It might not change the sex ratio of the district drastically, and the mindsets of people will take years to change, but this is one way of telling our girls that we need them, and they are indispensable in our lives," Dr. Pawar said.

Hindu and Buddhist spiritual traditions involve the belief in reincarnation, in an afterlife, in Karma and Dharma, in the soul being continuously reborn into a higher or lower caste based on its conduct in previous lives on earth, before it can finally ascend to Nirvana, and thus achieving release from the painful cycle of rebirth and human living. Souls returning to this life as women are deemed to have been deficient in some way in an earlier life, rebirth as a woman being a rebirth inferior to that of a man – a religious underpinning to the notion that women are inferior and unequal to men. In Buddhism, women must attain rebirth as men before they could pursue the path that would lead to perfect Buddhahood.

Buddhism is an extension or outgrowth of Hinduism. It was founded by Siddharta Gautama, the Buddha, who had lived the earlier portion of his life as a Hindu. When he started teaching Buddhism, it gained traction partly because even though it maintained some important tenets of the original, it did however, abandon other significant aspects such as the caste system and the religious authority of the Brahmins. Women and the lower castes were attracted to Buddhism precisely because it challenged the inequalities of the Hindu-based caste system and its patriarchal notions. In Buddhism, it is sometimes claimed, neither caste nor gender was considered an impediment to enlightenment, but, in the Pali Canon, it is reported, Gautama Buddha himself declared, that it is impossible that a woman should be "the perfectly rightfully Enlightened One, the Universal Monarch, the Kind of Gods, the Kind of Death or Brahmaa" – the Five Obstacles that women, only, face.

In the Chinese Buddhist traditions, including Confucianism, women occupy the same lower rungs of the society. Despite changes in Chinese philosophies for living such as that described by Mao Tse Tung's famed political slogan, "Women Hold Up Half The Sky," "women did not achieve equality with men, nor did they attain egalitarian self-determination nor social autonomy," writes Michael Wielink. "Nevertheless," he also wrote, "when Chinese Communism under Chairman Mao is analyzed we discover women, both rural and urban, were able to challenge social, cultural, and economic gender stratification. Mao envisaged "women's equality" as a dynamic force with an indelible power to help build a Chinese Communist State."

Today, in both India and China, femicide continues to threaten the lives of babies who are girls. The thinking continues to be that, girls – of course, not educated or allowed any autonomy to build lives for themselves – bring more cost than value to families and communities, so babies born female continue to be murdered at alarming rates.

One woman, visiting China in recent years as a social researcher, recounts having been present at a birth in a rural Chinese village. The baby, found to be female, was, quite simply, tossed into the bucket along with afterbirth and excreta, to be dumped into the cesspit on the family compound.

The reality is, however, that women do make up half of the population of the world. The reality is that women do contribute considerably to human living. The reality is that women are still actively – and foolishly, injudiciously and irresponsibly – being actively prevented from contributing anything even close to their capacity. This obtains despite the mountains of objective and incontrovertible evidence that the inclusion of women in the processes of the society, and in the public spaces and activities, boosts socio-cultural progress and drives economic development.

It is glaringly obvious in the modern histories of many countries, yet the resistance persists worldwide. The countries that are suffering the most, that are stagnant or that are "failed", persist in that condition in large part because the majority of actors, and sometimes, the only actors, on their leadership stages are men. These are the countries which choose to ignore the evidence, or are unable to comprehend the simple notion that it is difficult to advance if only half of the skills and potential available is being utilised, or that progress and development, not to mention economic prosperity, are aided by the inclusion of women. These are the countries that continue to sacrifice individual lives and community livelihoods to, not merely unhelpful, but outright destructive ideals of manhood and male supremacy.

Of course, the arguments that women's sovereignty results in the breakdown of some aspects of family and community structure, and in the abandonment of some traditions, are very valid, in some instances. And that is as it should be, in many of those instances. It is clear that there are a multitude of these aspects and traditions that are unjust, damaging, destructive, unenlightened and unhelpful and should, in the interest of every sector of society, be broken down, abandoned and dispensed with, forthwith. The reality for our societies, though, is that the "breakdown" that is actually being most fervently resisted, is that one which results in the dismantling of the ancient, antediluvian, outmoded structures of male power, privilege and supremacy – the patriarchy.

It never has been that any group willingly and easily gives up power, privilege or supremacy, and it probably never will be. The challenge for us all, therefore, lies in finding ways to demonstrate to and convince men that they, themselves, gain far more than they lose when women are engaged and involved and participating fully in all sectors of society. It rests with all of us who know to persuade and satisfy men that they, themselves, individually and in their groups, their work and their aspirations and opportunities, are supported, strengthened and enhanced when women are unhindered and unimpeded, and that though novel and unfamiliar, the exchange would be immeasurably more valuable than any privilege they might conceivably lose in the process.

When Hillary Clinton was Secretary of State for the United States, she was heard on several occasions to lament that in her higher-level meetings, she was often the only woman in the room. She believes that women need to be in the rooms and chairs of leadership, powerbroking and decision-making.

Chancellor Angela Merkel of Germany, has lived a similar experience. The European Union and the world have borne witness to the accomplishments afforded her own country and the rest of the world by her presence and contributions in those rooms, and by the general acknowledgment that even in those circumstances she has "always remained true to herself." Working with what little was available to her in her war-ravaged country, Liberia, Ellen Johnson-Sirleaf managed anyway to keep that country on an even keel, precisely because she was a woman in the decision-making rooms of Liberia and the African community of nations.

Tsai Ing-wen, serving as the 7th President of Taiwan, is leading a highly-industrialised country that is, anyhow, part of a system that is not only heavily male but is also philosophically and socially Confucian. Confucianism holds to the 'three submissions' which means that 'while not married, a woman submits to her father; when married, she submits to her husband; when her husband is dead, she submits to her son'. The leadership of the People's Republic of China broke off official communication with Taiwan after Dr. Tsai first won election in 2016, making her the first woman to ascend to the office of Head of State of that country.

At a high-level meeting in the capital of Chile in 2015, women leaders and experts from around the world reaffirmed that women's participation in decision-making is highly beneficial, and that women's role in designing and applying public policies has a positive impact on people's lives and communities.

The conference, themed *"Women in power and decision-making: Building a different world"*, was organised by UN Women and the Chilean government. It was led by then Chilean President Michelle Bachelet, who is a former head of UN Women, and Phumzile Mlambo-Ngcuka of South Africa, the current Executive Director of UN Women.

"There is already enough evidence in the world to show the positive impact of women's leadership. Women have successfully built and run countries and cities, economies and formidable institutions," said Mlambo-Ngcuka.

Tarcila Rivera, a Peruvian journalist and activist for the rights of indigenous women, told Inter Press Service (IPS) that when assessing the progress made in the last two decades, "it should be made clear that we have advanced but have only closed some gaps."

The presence and contributions of women improve systems – political, social, economic and all others. Women bring intelligence, intuition, empathy and highly-developed communication skills among many other gifts. The best leadership of a world that is better than we have had recently will require that women and men complement and are complemented by the skills, proficiencies, ambitions, rights and freedoms that each group brings.

It cannot naturally be that men or women alone are competent at any one thing. It cannot any longer be considered sensible or practical to ignore the capacity and value that women have so amply demonstrated that they bring. It cannot possibly be considered wise or safe to continue to deny improvement to communities and countries and deprive them of prosperity, just so as to be able to hold on to questionable and antediluvian notions of social arrangement.

In a presentation to a Forum on Public Policy, Leah Witcher Jackson, Associate Dean and Professor of Law, Baylor University School of Law, said that, no country can fully develop economically and socially if it fails to tap and fully utilize the talent of its citizens, half of which are women.

"A growing body of research and a growing number of organizations and governments recognize that focusing on women and girls is the most effective way to fight global poverty and extremism," she said. "The world is awakening to a powerful truth that not only are women and girls not the problem, but they may, in fact, very well be the solution."

Winnie Byanyima, executive director of Oxfam International, told IPS, "It is not about men against women, but there is evidence to show, through research, that when you have more women in public decision-making, you get policies that benefit women, children and families in general." Families include men and boys. She also reiterated that, when they're in parliament, for example, women tend to promote women's rights legislation. When women are in sufficient numbers in parliaments they also promote children's rights and they tend to speak up more for the interests of communities – local communities – because of their close involvement in community life.

Women know that life is made easier all across the board and for everyone when women are not restricted in their ability to contribute. The data is very clear in every sector. Slowly, but surely, and reassuringly, more and more men, also, are discovering this every day. That bodes well.

Women bring great value to every sector of human living. That is a given. It has been demonstrated and proven ad infinitum despite obstacles, denials and disavowals. The infinite possibilities of human living are denied to all of humanity as long as the greatest possibilities and highest potential of women continue to be denied expression and engagement.

The relationship between the quality of human living and the quality and extent of the involvement and engagement of women is one of direct proportionality

– the one rises as the other does and stagnates as long as the other is forced to. The solution is clear. The solution is practical. The solution is the equality of women generally, and the inclusion of women in positions of leadership in every sector of human living, without obstruction.

Women have the right to not be obstructed in either the development or exercise of individual capabilities and competencies. Women have the right to participate and contribute to the general good without let or hindrance.

Women have proven, time and time again, that we have the ability to contribute to the general good across all sectors of human living. Women have proven, time and time again, that we have the ability to lead at the very highest levels. Women bring great value to the world.

In equality of opportunity lies the fulfilment of the potential and promise of women, for the benefit of the entirety of humanity.

In equality of value lies the fulfilment of the potential and promise of the entirety of humanity.

FYI

If they don't *give you a seat* at the *table,*
bring a folding *chair.*"
-   Congresswoman Shirley Chisholm

The Pew Research Center reported in 2017, that in Zimbabwe, Malawi, the Gambia, Liberia and Tanzania, women account for at least 50% of the officially recognized workforce.

In most European Union countries, the labour force is at least 45% female. Malta, with 38.6%, is the most notable exception.

The six countries with the smallest shares of female workers are the Palestinian territories, Algeria, Iran, Saudi Arabia, Syria and Qatar. Israel, with 47.3%, is the only country in the Middle East where women account for more than 35% of the labour force.

Bhutan at 46.7% and Kazakhstan with 48.8% are in the top half of the countries examined, and the female share of the labour force in these countries roughly matches or exceeds the female share in the U.S.

Like the U.S., Bhutan and Kazakhstan, Canada has a relatively high proportion of women in the workforce, 47.3%. Five countries in the Western Hemisphere have an even larger percentage of female workers, though: French Guiana, an overseas region of France has 48.0%;

Bermuda and the Cayman Islands, both British Overseas Territories in the Caribbean, have 48.7% and 48.8% respectively, while two independent Caribbean nations, the Bahamas and Barbados, have 49.5% and 49.7% respectively.

Catalyst, a not-for profit organisation focused on women in the workplace, cites a 2020 analysis of over 1,100 organizations across the world which reports on the numbers and percentages of women in leadership. Those figures are: executives 23%, senior managers 29%, managers 37%, professionals 42% and support staff 47%.

The Council on Foreign Relations says that as of September 2020, only 22 out of 193 countries in the world have a female head of state. Of those 193 countries, 173 have a government that is less than 50% female, and some countries have not even one woman in their officers of government.

WAR AND PEACE

WHEN WOMEN LEAD

56

Women are not at the peace table…
our sensitivities to human needs, human rights
are sorely needed.
\- Margarita Chant Papandreou

According to the Global Peace Index (GPI), produced by the Institute for Economics and Peace since 2006, there were only 10 countries free from armed conflict in 2016 - Botswana, Chile, Costa Rica, Japan, Mauritius, Panama, Qatar, Switzerland, Uruguay and Vietnam.

Iceland remains the most peaceful country in the world, a position it has held since 2008. It is joined at the top of the index by New Zealand, Austria, Portugal, and Denmark.

The International Business Times and other sources place the United States and Russia at the top of the list of countries involved in conflict.

Violence costs 13.3% of world GDP, or $1,876 US for each person in the world.

Peacefulness has declined 2.5 percent since 2008, with 81 GPI countries recording a deterioration, and 79 improving. Fifteen of the 23 GPI indicators are less peaceful on average in 2020 when compared to 2008.

The results for 2020 show that the average country peacefulness score has fallen by 0.34 per cent. This is the ninth deterioration in peacefulness in the last twelve years, with 81 countries improving, and 80 recording deteriorations over the past year.

The 2020 GPI reveals a world in which the conflicts and crises that emerged in the past decade have begun to abate, only to be replaced with a new wave of tension and uncertainty as a result of the COVID-19 pandemic.

Afghanistan is the least peaceful country in the world for the second year in a row, followed by Syria, Iraq, South Sudan and Yemen.

The report for 2020 also looks at the trends in civil unrest over the past decade. It finds that there has been a sharp increase in civil unrest events since 2011, with over 96 countries experiencing at least one violent demonstration in 2019.

From 2011 to 2019, the number of riots rose by 282 per cent and general strikes rose by 821 per cent. Europe had the largest number of protests, riots and strikes over the period, totalling nearly 1,600 events from 2011 to 2018.

Sixty-five per cent of the civil unrest events in Europe in that period were nonviolent.

Europe remains the most peaceful region in the world, although it has recently recorded a slight deterioration in peacefulness. The region is home to 13 of the 20 most peaceful countries, and only two European countries are not ranked in the top half of the index.

Civil unrest in sub-Saharan Africa rose by more than 800 percent over the period, from 32 riots and protests in 2011, to 292 in 2018.

The only GPI region not to experience an increase in civil unrest from 2011 to 2018 was the

Middle East and North Africa, with total civil unrest events falling 60 per cent over that period. However, 2011 was the height of the Arab Spring in the region, with protests and demonstrations turning into open conflict and civil war in some countries, most notably in Syria.

Violence continues to have a significant impact on economic performance around the globe.

In the ten countries most affected by violence, the average economic impact of violence was equivalent to 41 per cent of GDP on average, compared to under 4 per cent in the countries least affected by violence.

The total number of natural disasters has tripled in the last four decades, while their economic impact has also increased.

Climate change is expected to create up to 86 million additional migrants in sub-Saharan Africa, 40 million in South Asia and 17 million in Latin America, by 2050.

More than two billion people already live in countries experiencing high levels of water stress.

An UNCTAD report published in November, 2020, warns that a viable COVID-19 vaccine will not halt the spread of economic damage, which will be felt long into the future, especially by the poorest and most vulnerable of the world.

HOWEVER

63

MANY WOMEN IN LEADERSHIP
=
SAFER COUNTRIES

…governments composed of men…,
have declared war on one another.
The women…have not been consulted …
- Harriette Beanland, 1914, 3 days after WWI declared

The African country of Liberia has endured two civil wars in recent history. The first lasted from 1989 until 1997, the second from 1999 'til 2003. The 1st Liberian Civil War ended with the general elections in 1997 in which Charles Taylor took power. After a rebellion and two coups, one successful and one not, and a civil war estimated to have killed more than a quarter of a million of Liberia's people, Taylor became President. This was he, who, a former minister of the government of Liberia, had somehow managed to escaped from a maximum-security federal prison in the United States of America, the Plymouth County Correctional Facility in The Commonwealth of Massachusetts, in 1985, returned to Liberia in 1989 with a militia, and set off the war.

During Taylor's time as president, more than 50,000 people were killed, thousands more were tortured and mutilated, and whole countries very seriously harmed. Charles Taylor helped finance the Revolutionary United Front, which inflicted mayhem immeasurable on the citizens of Sierra Leone. His militia were known to rape women, amputate people's limbs, enslave survivors of their attacks, kidnap and force boys into child armies, force boys to do unspeakable things to their family members.

Rape was a weapon of war utilised without restraint in that conflict, say reporters. Leymah Gbowee concurs. Interviewed about a documentary on the Liberia of those times, entitled, *Pray the Devil back to Hell,* Gbowee, one of the leaders of Liberian women's resistance to Taylor, said, "There is no other description…That was the life we lived…You wake up in the morning and you're just wondering…am I going to get shot as I walk the streets? Is my younger brother going to be conscripted? Am I going to be raped?"

"Early morning," she recounted, "someone comes to you and says, "Remember your classmate you graduated with three months ago? This morning, the entire family was slaughtered." Those were the kinds of things you grew up with…Death, at one point, was better than life."

Under Taylor's iron rule, civil war broke out again Liberia in 1999. In 2003, he was forced to resign, and went into exile in Nigeria. Liberia's new President, Ellen Johnson-Sirleaf, made a formal request for his extradition.

Charles Taylor was tried through the Special Court for Sierra Leone and the International Criminal Court. He was found guilty of the eleven charges brought against him and sentenced to fifty years in jail. The reaction of the Government of Sierra Leone was that the sentence was "a step forward as justice has been done, though the magnitude of the sentence is not commensurate with the atrocities committed".

Charles Taylor is imprisoned in Her Majesty's Prison Frankland in the United Kingdom.

During the Taylor years, Leymah Gbowee helped her country women to form an organization called, "Women of Liberia Mass Action for Peace". She brought together more than three thousand Liberian women, including Christians and Muslims, and together, they staged years of non-violent protests around the country. The women dressed all in white, white being used in many places as a symbol of women's political resistance, and some of their resistance events were silent protests in front of the Presidential buildings.

Despairing about an end to the violence and war, and desperate for peace, Women of Liberia Mass Action for Peace eventually settled on an unorthodox strategy to bring the men around to their point – they asked the women of Liberia to go on a sex strike until their men agreed to put their weapons down and end the war.

"No peace, no sex." Gbowee has been reported as saying that even though her suggestion was not necessarily put into practice, the threat alone proved useful in "getting people's attention".

The activism of Gbowee and the women of Mass Action for Peace forced Taylor to agree to attend peace talks in Ghana, then showed up in Accra to keep the pressure on. Gbowee's website tells us that she led the delegation of women to Accra, to ensure progress was made. At a crucial moment, when the talks seemed to be stalling, Leymah and about two hundred other women entered the hotel where the men were meeting, sat on the floor and linked arms, forming a human barricade so as to prevent Taylor's representatives and the rebel warlords from leaving the meeting hall for food or any other reason, until they reached a peace agreement.

News stories of the day report that security forces tried to arrest the women, but Leymah and some of the women threatened to undress and take their clothes all off, right there, in public. The soldiers were shocked and dismayed. They fell back in utter consternation.

"She displayed tactical brilliance in threatening to disrobe," says her website, "an act that according to traditional beliefs would have brought a curse of terrible misfortune upon the men" for being witness to the nakedness of their "mothers".

"I will make it easier for you," she told the security guards. "I'll strip naked, so that when you take me to prison, it will be easier. "So, by the time I had started taking my clothes off," she later recounted in a television interview with Jon Stewart, "maybe they were afraid of what they would see, [but] they all ran away."

The women's threat worked, and it proved to be a decisive turning point for the peace process. The Accra Comprehensive Peace Agreement was signed very shortly thereafter and the Liberian war was officially brought to an end. Within weeks, Taylor resigned the presidency and went into exile, the peace treaty having also mandated that a transitional government be set up for Liberia.

Ellen Johnson-Sirleaf was elected leader of the country in 2005 on the powerful commitment of women who had seen the war perpetrated and perpetuated by men in their country, and who were unwilling to put a man back into that powerful role right then. Sirleaf became the first woman president of the country, and the first woman elected head of state on the entire continent of Africa. In 2011, she and Gbowee were awarded a joint Nobel Peace Prize for their work.

Liberia is still a poor and struggling country where corruption, illiteracy and unemployment are proving difficult to root out, but the times of war have ended and according to the UNDP, the country is now recorded as one of the fourteen countries with the highest gain in the Human Development Index (HDI). The HDI is a summary measure of average achievement in key dimensions of human development: a long and healthy life, being knowledgeable, and having a decent standard of living. Liberia is experiencing an increase of about two percent a year.

In 2014, as Rwanda marked the 20th anniversary of the genocide, an editorial in the New York Times hailed the country as "an island of order and relative prosperity in a poor and politically volatile region."

A New York Times article of April 2019, reads: Twenty-five years ago, on April 7, 1994, the dominant Hutus of Rwanda turned with well-planned violence on the Tutsi minority whom they held to be traitors. One hundred days later, when the killing finally stopped, the death toll stood at as many as one million, mostly Tutsis but also including some moderate Hutus who had opposed the bloodletting. Women suffered untold rapes and gang rapes, accelerating the spread of AIDS. The offspring of these assaults were stigmatized as "children of the killers".

As a direct consequence of the killings of and by men in the genocide of 1994, the population of Rwanda is now mostly women. With sixty-one point three percent of its members being female, the composition of the parliament reflects the male to female ratio in the country. While President Paul Kagame has been successful at maintaining order in the country, he is also accused of having a very heavy hand, stifling dissent and locking up women who dare challenge him for the Presidency. Still, it is the general consensus that the high proportion of women in leadership in parliament and all the other sectors across the society are one of the reasons why Rwanda is continuing to heal and reconcile, and is not likely to descend into any comparable state of darkness any time soon.

According to the British Broadcasting Corporation, BBC, until the 19th century, Britain and the other European powers had confined their imperial ambitions, in Africa, to the odd coastal outpost from which they could exert their economic and military influence. Between 1562 and 1807, when the slave trade was abolished, says the BBC, British ships carried up to three million people into slavery in the Americas. In total, European ships took more than 11 million people into slavery from the West African coast, and European traders grew rich on the profits while the population of Africa's west coast was devastated.

Also according to the BBC, "One of the chief justifications for the so-called 'scramble for Africa' which occurred roughly between the years 1884 and 1914, when the men who governed the European colonizer countries took it upon themselves to partition the continent into protectorates, colonies and 'free-trade zones' was a desire to stamp out slavery once and for all. Livingstone put forward the theory, apparently, that the only way to liberate Africa, from the horrors of slavery and exploitation, was to introduce the 'three Cs': commerce, Christianity and civilisation.

In truth, however, the strategic and economic objectives of the colonial powers, such as protecting old markets and exploiting new ones, were far more important. BBC also records that, "Commercial greed, territorial ambition, and political rivalry all fuelled the European race to take over Africa."

South African History Online's Grade 8, Term 3 lesson on The Scramble for Africa, teaches that, "In 1884, at the request of Portugal, German Chancellor Otto von Bismark called together the major western powers of the world to negotiate questions and end their confusion over the control of Africa. The countries represented at the time included AustriaHungary, Belgium, Denmark, France, Germany, Great Britain, Italy, the Netherlands, Portugal, Russia, Spain, Sweden-Norway (unified from 1814-1905), Turkey, and the United States of America.

Of these fourteen nations, France, Germany, Great Britain, and Portugal were the major players in the conference, controlling most of colonial Africa at the time. Britain, France, Germany, Belgium, Italy, Portugal, and Spain were competing for power within European power politics.

They would meet in Berlin, for what would come to be called variously, the Berlin Conference, the Congo

Conference, or the West Africa Conference. Africa was not included in the meeting.

"The only clue as to the purpose of the November (1884) gathering of white men," writes Al Jazeera, was a map of Africa hung on the wall, "drooping down like a question mark" in the words of Nigerian historian, Professor Godfrey Uzoigwe. What ultimately resulted from rules of conquest and partition that were set during the three-and-a-half month long meeting, was "a hodgepodge of geometric boundaries that divided Africa into fifty irregular countries," and has left a legacy of seemingly intractable political fragmentation, tribal conflict, corruption, exploitation, devastation and violence.

On the website History.com is written: World War I, also known as the Great War, began in 1914 after the assassination of Archduke Franz Ferdinand of Austria, in Sarajevo, the capital of Bosnia. He and his wife, Sophie, Duchess of Hohenburg, were shot by the nineteen-year-old Serbian nationalist Gavrilo Princip who, with other nationalists was struggling to end Austro-Hungarian rule over Bosnia and Herzegovina.

The assassination unleashed a series of events that catapulted Europe into a war which lasted until 1918. During the conflict, Germany, Austria-Hungary, Bulgaria and the Ottoman Empire (the Central Powers) fought against Great Britain, France, Russia, Italy, Romania, Japan and the United States (the Allied Powers). Thanks to new – at the time – military technologies and the horrors of trench warfare, World War I saw unprecedented levels of carnage and destruction. By the time the war was over and the Allied Powers claimed victory, more than 16 million people – soldiers and civilians alike – were dead.

History.com also teaches that, "the instability created in Europe by the First World War set the stage for another international conflict – World War II – which broke out two decades later, and would prove even more devastating. Rising to power in an economically and politically unstable Germany, Adolf Hitler, leader of the Nazi Party, rearmed the nation and signed strategic treaties with Italy and Japan to further his ambitions of world domination.

Hitler's invasion of Poland in September 1939, drove Great Britain and France to declare war on Germany, marking the beginning of World War II. Over the next six years, the conflict would take more lives and destroy more land and property around the globe than any previous war. Among the estimated 45-60 million people killed were 6 million Jews murdered in Nazi concentration camps as part of Hitler's diabolical "Final Solution," now known as the Holocaust.

The word "Holocaust," from the Greek words "holos" (whole) and "kaustos" (burned), was historically used to describe a sacrificial offering burned on an altar. Since 1945, the word has taken on a new and horrible meaning. It now refers, almost exclusively, says History.com, to the ideological and systematic state-sponsored persecution and mass murder of millions of European Jews (as well as millions of others, including Romani people, the intellectually disabled, political dissidents and homosexuals, targeted for racial, political, ideological or behavioural reasons) by the German Nazi regime between 1933 and 1945. More than one million of those who perished were children.

The "Palestinian Territories" is a term that has been used for many years now, to refer to the territories occupied by Israel since 1967, within what was, immediately prior to that called, the British Mandate for Palestine after Britain, and before that Ottoman Syria. The Council on Foreign Relations says that, "The Israeli-Palestinian conflict dates back to the end of the 19th century. In 1947, the United Nations adopted Resolution 181, the Partition Plan, which sought to divide the British mandate of Palestine into Arab and Jewish states. On May 14th, 1948, the State of Israel was Created, sparking the first Arab-Israeli War."

The violence and conflict have never ended. They continue unabated, to this day, kept alive by, among other things, an Israeli policy of evictions of Palestinians from traditional lands, Israeli control of Palestinian resources, Palestinian resistance, retaliation and intifadas, religious zealotry, community anguish and individual pain, and entrenched inflexibility and unyieldingness.

Forbes Magazine noted in an article published after one recent surge of violence in that war, entitled, *Israeli*

And Palestinian Women: The Only Way Is Together, "Although the violence has stopped and people worldwide have moved on to the next trending international crisis, Israelis, Palestinians, and their families in the diaspora continue to suffer the consequences of living in a constant state of war."

Over a period of three months, ForbesWomen journalists interviewed Israelis and Palestinians living in Israel, the Palestinian Territories and the diaspora, and organisations who work with the goal of promoting coexistence among the two peoples, and bringing Israelis and Palestinians together.

"Oftentimes, though," the article goes on to say, "the hate and noise overshadow voices that call for equality, peace and unity. These voices advocate for a future where Israelis and Palestinians, two groups of people with historical ties to the same land, can live among and next to each other, break bread together, with equal protection, rights and without a border and separation wall.

"These voices believe coexistence and understanding is the only way for an equitable future for Israelis and Palestinians – and many leading this fight are women."

Forbes says that the women interviewed are working both independently and as part of non-profit and other organisations, to bridge gaps and break down walls, literally and figuratively, and build a world in which the two peoples are not enemies, but neighbours and friends.

The website of the Women's International League of Peace and Freedom declares that the League addresses "the root causes of violence through a feminist lens". The website also says that on 28 April 1915, during World War I, a unique group of 1,136 women from warring and neutral nations gathered in The Hague, the Netherlands, to discuss how to end the war and ensure permanent peace. They believed that the full and equal participation of women in the decision-making processes was necessary to achieve sustainable peace. The meeting ended with the foundation of the Women's International League of Peace and Freedom. Out of these beginnings, Peace Women was instituted in the year 2000. Formally named the Women, Peace and Security Programme, it was founded "to strengthen women's rights and participation in international peace and security efforts."

In 2014, Peace Women hosted *Women's Action For Peace: Prospects and Challenges for Women in the MENA (Middle East and North Africa),* one day in advance of the High-level Forum on the Culture of Peace at the UN headquarters in New York. The delegates included women from Sudan, Palestine, Egypt, Libya, Somalia and other countries of the MENA region.

A publication from Germany's Federal Ministry for Economic Cooperation and Development titled *Enhancing Women's Leadership for Sustainable Peace in Fragile Contexts in the MENA Region,* says,

"Women's participation in peace processes is crucial for the effectiveness of peace and security initiatives. Research shows the links between women's inclusion and the likelihood of more durable and stable peace."

An analysis conducted by the Graduate Institute Geneva, of forty peace processes agreed to since 1989, shows that in cases where women's groups were able to exercise strong influence on the negotiation process, chances were higher that an agreement would be reached than when women's groups exercised weak or no influence. The strong influence of women on negotiation processes also positively correlated with a greater likelihood of agreements being implemented.

In a 2018 study reported in the journal International Interactions, in the section *Empirical and Theoretical Research in International Relations*, the researchers write, "We have shown that women's participation in peace negotiations with voice and influence, leads to better accord content, higher agreement implementation rates, and longer lasting peace."

"As peacekeeping has evolved to reflect the populations we serve," says the UN, "women have become increasingly part of the peacekeeping family – making operations more effective. Our statistical results show a robust relationship between peace agreements with women signatories and peace durability. This relationship holds after controlling for conflict characteristics and the level of political and economic development, UN peacekeeping, the numbers of women in parliament and in rebel groups, gender quotas, and general civil society inclusion.

"We further find that peace agreements signed by women show a significantly higher number of agreement provisions and a higher implementation rate of these provisions than those not signed by women."

However, a 2016 special report from the United States Institutes of Peace notes that, "As conflicts in the region persist and economic inequality deepens, governments are prioritizing responses to the economic, political, and security crises in ways that preserve the status quo.

As a result, women are pushed to the periphery." United Nations Security Council Resolution (UNSCR) 1325 calls for the active participation of women in achieving peace and security through conflict resolution, conflict prevention and post-conflict management. The core pillars of the resolution are prevention, protection and participation. It also notes the importance of women in the preservation of international peace and security, and calls for their involvement on an equal basis with men, in dealing with peace and security issues.

Yet, all these years after the birth of UNSCR 1325 in 2000, its implementation is still hindered by underfunding and, confoundingly, by the marginalization of women, at a time when it is more important than ever to enlist women's talents in the cause of combating extremism and promoting peace, says a *Women, Peace and Security in the Middle East and North Africa Region* fact sheet compiled by Oxfam.

That fact sheet also says, "Women's leadership and participation in decision making is one of the fundamental building blocks for lasting peace and conflict prevention. Yet, despite the fact that UNSCR 1325 stresses the importance of women's participation in decision making, women's political participation remains low at national, regional and global levels.

"Donor countries," it also says, "invest billions of dollars in military security to counter violent extremism, but fail to allocate adequate resources to implement UNSCR 1325. This lack of political will to generate funding deprives the world of a very effective response to radicalization."

Women Wage Peace (WWP) was founded in the summer of 2014, and says it is the largest grassroots movement in Israel, whose purpose is to promote a political agreement involving women in the process. The movement has more than 44,000 members. WWP also says that the goal of the movement is "to bring about the resolution of the Israeli Palestinian conflict by means of an honourable, non-violent and mutually acceptable agreement, with the participation of women from diverse groups of the population in Israel."

The WWP say that they wage peace every day, and to that end, have held thousands of events in the years since their inception, from parlour meetings to fasts and protest walks. In 2015 they fasted for fifty days in tents outside the residence of the prime minister of Israel. In 2017, they organized a two-week protest walk of Israeli and Palestinian activists through parts of Israel and the West Bank, ending with a rally in Jerusalem to demand a peace deal.

The Times of Israel reports Huda Abuarquob, one of the organizers and a Palestinian from Hebron in the West Bank, as saying, "This march is not just another protest, but a way of saying that we want peace, and together we can obtain it."

Women Wage Peace says, "We are not stopping until there is an agreement."

Back in 2000, when he was Secretary-General of the United Nations, Kofi Annan stressed that maintaining and promoting peace and security required women's equal participation in decision-making. Women had proved instrumental, he said, in "building bridges rather than walls". They had also been crucial in preserving social order when communities collapsed. "In all these areas, we have seen examples of women playing an important role", he said.

"We cannot silence the guns in Africa without the inclusion of women in peace processes," remarked African Union Special Envoy Bineta Diop, speaking at the virtual African Forum on Women, Peace and Security in November, 2020. Africa now has 30 countries with National Action Plans for the implementation of the Women, Peace and Security agenda.

"Gender equality is a strong predictor of a state's peacefulness and development," Espinosa Garces,

Ecuadorian politician and diplomat and the 2018-2019 President of the UN General Assembly, has said. "We have proven that where women are more empowered, a state is less likely to experience civil conflict or go to war."

Despite all of the ever-rising mountains of evidence of women's capabilities and successes in maintaining peace and security and keeping communities and countries safe, women's involvement in these sectors is still severely undervalued. The decision-making in these matters is still, distressingly, overwhelmingly male, and overwhelmingly militaristic in attitude and approach.

"I am convinced that the women of the world, united without any regard for national or racial dimensions, can become a most powerful force for international peace and brotherhood," was the position of Coretta Scott-King, widow of Dr. Martin Luther King Jr.

For the most part, the men who rule the world seem not to agree.

82

83

MANY WOMEN IN LEADERSHIP
=
HEALTHIER POPULATIONS

84

To handle yourself, use your head;
to handle others, use your heart.
-       Eleanor Roosevelt

Irene Archos, is a writer/blogger/journalist, educator, expressive arts workshop leader, photographer and encaustic artist who uses the code name: Greek-American Girl. She describes herself as "bursting with creative energy which is what I bring to whatever endeavor I spark. I am especially interested in using creativity to heal, in the service of health."

She wrote about Agnodice in one blog post, with the comment, "Of course, history, male dominated, can do the worst injustice to Agnodice's case. It can try to erase her. The case has been made that she never existed."

Agnodice is written about in *Fabulae* by the Roman author Gaius Julius Hyginus, and observes Greek-American Girl, "Had it not been for Hyginus, we would not have known about this remarkable woman who broke all rules and became a living legend in her day…proving the maxim that "good girls don't make history." In Agnodice's time, women were forbidden from practising medicine. It is said that, Hippocrates, called the father of medicine, had allowed and even encouraged women to study medicine, midwifery, and obstetrics, but Agnodice is said to have lived in Athens, a city-state that was patriarchal to its core.

The rulers of Athens made it illegal for women to be doctors and so, the story goes, this young woman disguised herself as a man in order to get accepted into "medical school" in Alexandria. When she completed her studies, she returned to Athens, still disguised as a man, and began her work as a gynecologist.

"Now can you imagine the agony," asks Greek-American Girl, "the outright terror of being a young woman in ancient times in Athens, a most patriarchal city, who had to suffer exams by male physicians who either had no understanding or no sympathy for female biology. She…was horrified at the numbers of women who were bleeding to death, who suffered through early miscarriage, or otherwise were treated like heifers by a male-only medical establishment."

The women of Athens, comforted and reassured by this sensitive, new doctor, were flocking to her. They kept her secret well, but of course, the 'deception' could have lasted only so long. Eventually, the male physicians got jealous, accused the young "man" of underhanded dealings with men's wives, and hauled her before the Aeropagus. To defend herself, she lifted her tunic and showed that she was a woman and so could not have been capable of fathering children with the women.

The charges against her were changed, then, to practicing medicine as a woman. The women of Athens stormed the tribunal, reportedly, and demanded that she be freed and allowed to continue to work, and eventually the law was also changed to allow women into the medical profession.

Many scholars hold that Agnodice is a mythical figure, that she never actually existed. No one knows for sure, apparently, but the tale of Dr. Agnodice has been used by women since the 17th century, says Prof. Helen King, invoked as fact, and hence as a valuable past precedent, to defend themselves against a male-dominated medical profession seeking to medicalise childbirth. This could be considered more important, perhaps, than whether Agnodice actually existed or not.

Women are carers and caretakers by nature and/or by nurture. The main responsibility of a woman, therefore, many believe, is to preserve the human race. On this pretext, among others, the near-universal consensus has for centuries, been that a woman's place is in the home, at the hearth, barefoot and pregnant, and in the kitchen. Or working on the farm, toiling in the homestead, waiting in the harem. Or, as sometimes attributed to the French, a lady in the living room, a cook in the kitchen and a whore in the bedroom!

In societies across time and space, women have been socialized to be primarily the providers of care and maintenance to the family unit. Women are to do this by procuring, cooking and serving food, caring for dependent family members and by preparing children for productive adulthood. In societies across time and space, these all, in some combination, have been given as the primary reasons for women's existence.

The studies that have been conducted by Goodwin and others show that the contribution of women to the health of their families extends beyond that of food procurement and preparation, and into the responsibility for ensuring that dependent family members receive proper care of every kind. In some African and Caribbean societies, they report, the socialization process for preparing females to become the primary caretakers of their familial groups begins the minute girls are mobile and can understand instructions. It starts with them working alongside their mothers doing household chores and caring for siblings. Boys are generally not provided this training.

In families and communities, large and small, women play a central role, an essential and pivotal, though largely unacknowledged and in many ways, uncompensated role. By nature and/or because of the patriarchy, therefore, women have become, in many ways, the de facto fulcrum of the vast majority of families.

Thus, say Goodwin et al., in the International Journal of Global Health and Health Disparities, women's roles within families have positioned them to become health managers or promoters of overall family health. A model that utilizes women's roles within families to promote child and family health, therefore, is appropriate for women of all nations, they believe.

As food preparers, caretakers and the primary socializing agents, the roles of women within families are often synonymous, then, with health provider or family health manager. Along with other researchers and practitioners in the related sectors, Goodwin et al conclude that women essentially become *"producers of human capital"* because of their almost absolute decision-making influence. That influence contributes to the health of their children and their families, even extended families, as well as to their own health and ultimately to the health of the community and, it must follow, the ability to thrive of both the individual and the group.

The Organisation for Economic Co-operation and Development (OECD) defines human capital as "the knowledge, skills, competencies and other attributes embodied in individuals or groups of individuals, acquired during their life and used to produce goods, services or ideas in market circumstances".

"Human capital" encompasses the notion that investments are made in people – education, skills training, and health, for example – and that these investments increase an individual's productivity or capacity for production. Harvard University's Claudia Goldin thinks that the concept of human capital goes back at least to Adam Smith since his fourth definition of capital says that, "The acquisition of . . . talents during . . . education, study, or apprenticeship, costs a real expense, which is capital in [a] person. Those talents [are] part of his (sic) fortune [and] likewise that of society."

A 2012 master's thesis study conducted by Kathryn McGuigan in New Zealand "to explore the complexity of the mother's role across all areas of family health including food, sleep, exercise, medications, hygiene, health prevention such as immunisation, and safety, revealed that the mother's role as overseer of family health involved surveillance, provisioning and teaching, as well. In summary," McGuigan concludes, "therefore, the mother's role in family health is complex, multifaceted, and reflected in the family health philosophy." By extension, the family health is part and parcel of the national health. It is reported that Napoleon Bonaparte once said, "Give me good mothers and I will give you a good nation."

There is a book written by Dr. Jon Kabat-Zinn titled, *Wherever You Go, There You Are.* The book itself is about mindfulness, meditation and related concepts, but many people interpret the title to mean something along the lines of "shifting your physical location is not going to change who you are; no matter where you are or what you're doing, your basics don't change; you're always the same person with the same preferences, propensities and predispositions, no matter where you find yourself.

It would follow, that women are "the women they are" whether they are running their homes or operating elsewhere. Indeed, it must be obvious to even the most inattentive personalities that the same caretaking dynamics play out when women are active outside the home, for work or other any other reason else, and whatever the industry or the professional level. Neither is it by accident that the greatest portion of workers in the caregiving and "hospitality" sectors is women. The patriarchy and socialisation have colluded to create this condition, and it has been callously exploited by the economics of the world.

Out in the world of work, women tend to look after their colleagues very much in line with the rules of their domestic socialization. So, they mother their colleagues or act out big sister roles so much so that it had become quite necessary for women's magazines and leadership trainers to spend time advising women, newly active in the world of work created by men, to learn to step back a little from that and be more like the men – that is to say less chummy/friendly, more collegial/professional, less "helping" and more supportive, rather.

In the workplace, it is women who, whether they are leaders or line staff, are the ones who send around condolence and get-well cards, who organize baby showers and birthday surprises, who more readily offer to pick up the slack to support an ailing colleague, who ask about health and listen to the answers, who make hospital visits to sick colleagues – and who call to check up on them at home.

While male leaders are not necessarily any less interested in the health and wellbeing of colleagues and employees, studies do show that it is women team leaders, managers and executives who are more perceptive and responsive to things like burnout and other signs of distress. It is women colleagues who are more attentive to the emotional and psychological states of others and much more likely to offer advice and support – and referrals. In fact, on a related note, when marketing strategists at Reward Stream examined the potential for gender marketing strategies, the data indicated that women are twenty-five to thirty percent more likely than men to have referred people, companies and services.

A study undertaken by VOX-EU to consider whether and how the management of the COVID-19 pandemic was influenced in 2020 by the gender of a country's leader, confirms that female-led countries had fared better in terms of absolute number of COVID-19 cases and deaths, with male-led countries having nearly double the number of deaths as female-led ones.

However, the researchers say, drawing anything definitive or altogether conclusive from these raw comparisons is difficult due to the massive underrepresentation of female-led countries in the sample. There was only one sample available for their use – the only one that reflects the state of leadership in the world – with only nineteen countries across the world led by women, compared with the one hundred and seventy-four led by men.

"In a situation such as this, that pitted human life against economic outcomes," the writers say, "women leaders showed themselves significantly more risk averse in the domain of human life."

Calene Malek reported for ArabNews from the World Government Summit hosted virtually, in October 2020, by Abu Dhabi. In her article, she quotes Ohood Al-Roumi, the Minister of State for Government Development and the Future for the United Arab Emirates (UAE) as saying, "When you look at COVID-19, 70 percent of the front-liners fighting this pandemic are women. Countries who have more women in government senior leadership positions had better responses to the pandemic overall. Yet, women are about 39 percent of the global workforce in the world, and they occupy only 28 percent of managerial positions."

Malek also reports in the same piece that half the UAE's parliament is made up of women, compared to the global average of 25 percent, that one third of its (UAE) cabinet ministers are women in senior posts, and that women constitute two-thirds of university graduates and government employees. "More needs to be done around the world to enable and support more women to take more public leadership positions," said Al-Roumi. "To create a better world, the future is female."

The conclusion in this case is that COVID-19 outcomes are systematically and significantly better in countries led by women and, to some extent, this may be explained by the proactive policy responses they adopted. Even accounting for institutional context and other controls, being female-led has provided countries with an advantage in the crisis, i.e. they have suffered fewer cases of this disease and have remained healthier.

Three of the top ten healthiest countries in the world, according to the Bloomberg Global Health Index, are Iceland, Sweden, and Norway. The Scandinavian countries also have a long history of women in leadership. The CATO Institute writes that, "While Nordic societies are indeed role models when it comes to gender equality, this equality stretches back centuries before the modern welfare state and reflects traditional Nordic culture."

Related to that, the 2020 US News and World Report's list of the world's best countries for women, was once again topped by Scandinavian countries. Denmark, Sweden, Norway, and Finland were ranked among the top six. The Scandinavian model is largely seen as being perhaps the best example of support for female representation in the workplace. The reasons this is thought to be so include parity in political representation and inherent infrastructures such as crèches, day-care etc., maternity and paternity leave facilities, equal and pay policies.

To determine the world's most and least healthy countries, researchers at 24/7 Wall St. collected data on twenty-one measures in more than one hundred and seventy countries.

These measures were grouped into three categories: health, access and the economy. Information gathered from the World Bank and the World Health Organisation in the health category considered infant mortality, fertility, maternal mortality and the incidence of various diseases, smoking rates and the percentage of children with certain immunizations. The life expectancy figures for males was accepted as a proxy for life expectancies for all people because it is much more widely available in the countries reviewed. The group also considered per capita alcohol consumption and adult obesity rates.

The most healthy country in the world in 2020, according to these measures, was Spain. Interestingly, Spain has been making significant strides in recent years in the area of women's leadership. According to World Bank data, only Rwanda, Cuba, Bolivia and Mexico have higher female representation in parliament than does Spain, though this high level of representation has not yet registered a higher level of equity for women in other areas.

Spain has a larger proportion of female lawmakers than even Sweden which has a far longer history of promoting gender equality. In June 2018, Spain became the world's most female-centric government when incoming Prime Minister Pedro Sánchez swore-in a Cabinet that was roughly two-thirds female – eleven women to seven men.

One Spanish news site had lamented at one time that, "Only one Spaniard may have made it onto the 2015 list of Forbes 100 most powerful women, but there are many more Spanish women who are masters in their fields," and then went on to list ten, including Ana Botin who has been the executive chairperson of *Santander* Group since 2014; Ada Colau who rose from anti-austerity activist to become mayor of Barcelona; Edurne Pasaban who became the first woman to climb all fourteen of the mountains of the world that are higher than eight thousand metres; Isabel Coixet, one of the most famous contemporary Spanish film directors; Mireia Belmonte, swimmer, one of the most successful modern Spanish sportswomen; ballet dancer Tamara Rojo; Penelope Cruz, the most internationally successful Spanish actress of all time; and Margarita Salas, one of the most famous Spanish scientists in the world, renowned for her work in the fields of Biochemistry and Molecular genetics.

Despite having been born in Jamaica to an African mother at a time when the enslavement of African people was still legal, Mary Seacole was born a "free" person. In 1823, at the age of seventeen, she traveled on her own from Jamaica to London, England. She used the opportunity to acquire knowledge about modern European medicine, with which to supplement her training in traditional Caribbean techniques.

In 1844, Florence Nightingale enrolled as a nursing student at the Lutheran Hospital of Pastor Fliedner in

Kaiserwerth, Germany, determined to study what she considered her true calling, despite the objections of her parents.

The Crimean War broke out in 1853 and, says the BBC, newspaper reports from the front line told horror stories of the appalling conditions in British army hospitals. Soon after the start of the war, Seacole, having heard of the poor medical facilities for wounded soldiers, asked the British War Office to send her as an army nurse to the Crimea. The War Office refused her, so she funded her own voyage, arrived in Crimea and established the British Hotel to provide a place of respite for sick and convalescent officers. She also visited the battlefield, sometimes under fire, to nurse the wounded, even, on occasion, administering last rites to dying soldiers. She soon became known as 'Mother Seacole'. After the war she returned to England penniless and in poor health. The press highlighted her plight and in July 1857, a benefit festival organised to raise money for her, attracted thousands of people.

Sidney Herbert, Secretary of State at War, during the Crimean War, knew Florence Nightingale well, and in 1854, appointed her to take thirty-eight nurses to work in the military hospital in Scutari, Turkey. This became the first time that women were allowed to officially serve in the British army. When a portrait of Florence carrying a lamp and tending to patients appeared in the press, she became known as 'the Lady of the Lamp'.

After the war, with the backing of Queen Victoria, she persuaded the government to set up a Royal Commission into the health of the army. Often a lone female voice appealing to the Victorian establishment, her skill for communication and mathematics helped overhaul army and civilian healthcare and saved thousands from a gruesome death, say her historians. The legacy of leadership of these two remarkable women is evident in the eminently female nursing profession of today, in Britain and elsewhere.

Health is one of those "soft" areas into which women political leaders are routinely shunted, "hard" sectors such as energy, finance, mining and such like being overwhelmingly reserved for the men. So, Edwin Ng and Carles Muntaner, professors in social work and nursing respectively at the universities of Waterloo and Toronto, also respectively, took it upon themselves to examine whether there were an historical association between women in government and population health among Canada's ten provinces. What they found was that there was indeed a connection, and with deeper implications and far wider ramifications than might have been expected.

The data told them that between 1976 and 2009, the percentage of women in provincial government increased six-fold from 4.2 per cent to 25.9 per cent, while mortality from all causes declined by 37.5 per cent – from 8.85 to 5.53 deaths per 1000 people. Using data from provincial election offices and Statistics

Canada, they also found that as the average percentage of women in government has historically risen, total mortality rates have declined.

The two public health researchers write that when, in November 2015, Prime Minister Justin Trudeau formed the first gender-balanced cabinet in Canadian history, ensuring that half of his closest advisers were women, and Canada was vaulted from the twentieth to the fifth place in the world in terms of percentage of women in ministerial positions, it got them thinking — if increasing the number of women in positions of power promotes gender equity, could it also promote population health and well-being?

Their findings, published in the journal SSM - Population Health, support the argument that yes, women in government do in fact advance population health. This link does not, of course, mean that the increase of women in government has directly caused the decline in mortality, they are quick to clarify, but it does support the original hypothesis.

Interestingly, they also found that there was "no relationship between the political leanings of women in government whether they belonged to left-wing, centrist or right-wing parties, and mortality rates."

WHEN WOMEN LEAD

99

MANY WOMEN IN LEADERSHIP
=
DEEPER EMPATHY

*Leadership should be
more participative than directive,
more enabling than performing.*
-   Mary D. Poole

Empathy is often defined as the capacity to understand or feel what another person is experiencing, from within their particular frame of reference. Empathy is the capacity to place oneself in another person's position – in colloquial parlance, the ability to put oneself in someone else's shoes.

Writing in the Journal of Social Psychology, Loren Roussaint and Jon R. Webb assert that much research has shown that women are more empathic than men. Citing a variety of sources, they write that the broad definition of *empathy* includes affective and cognitive components, that empathy has been defined as "accurately perceiving the internal frame of reference of another", and includes nonverbal communication.

They refer to B.S. Moore's assertion that empathy is "an organizer and regulator of a variety of behaviours" and quote Zahn-Waxler and Radke-Yarrow that empathy is central to what it means to be fully human. As such, they find, empathy is critical to moral development and justice, thereby acting as a catalyst for societal cohesion and unity, because constructive interpersonal relations are contingent upon a willingness to take another's perspective, which women do more often and better than men.

The Greater Good Science Center at University of California, Berkeley, teaches that empathy is a broad topic covering a wide range of experiences. Researchers into emotion generally define empathy as the ability to sense other people's emotions, coupled with the ability to imagine what someone else might be thinking or feeling – and there are worlds of nuance in that.

It is important to clarify that empathy and sympathy are not the same thing. They are often confused. Sympathy is a feeling of pity or sorrow. Dr. Neel Burton, a British psychiatrist and author of books that include *Heaven and Hell: The Psychology of the*

Emotions, writes that sympathy, 'fellow feeling' or 'community of feeling, "is a feeling of care and concern for someone, often someone close, accompanied by a wish to see that person better off or happier. Unlike empathy, sympathy does not involve a shared perspective or shared emotions, and while the facial expressions of sympathy do convey caring and concern, they do not convey shared distress."

It seems to be generally agreed that there are three types of empathy: cognitive, emotional and compassionate. Psychologists Daniel Goleman and Paul Ekman define the three types as follows: cognitive empathy, the ability to understand how a person feels and what they might be thinking. Cognitive empathy makes us better communicators, because it helps us relay information in a way that best reaches the other person; emotional empathy, also referred to as affective empathy, means that a person is able to share the feelings of another person. Some have described it as "your pain in my heart."

This type of empathy helps people build emotional connections with others; and compassionate empathy, also known as empathic concern, which goes beyond simply understanding others and sharing their feelings. It actually moves us to take action, to help however we can.

Dr. David Olmos believes that the degree to which a person actually feels another person's pain might depend on the sex of the empathiser. Dr. Leonardo Christov-Moore, a UCLA postdoctoral fellow in psychiatry and biobehavioral sciences, and Dr. Marco

Iacoboni, director of the Neuromodulation Lab at the UCLA Ahmanson-Lovelace Brain Mapping Center, conducted a study on the brain activity of people as they reacted to images of pain in others and then reported their key findings. *"One of the foundational skills for being a competent social agent is empathy,"* the doctors say, and women have more of it. And that's not exactly news. Community wisdom has long said this of women, and community wisdom often contains much more than a grain of truth.

Says Dr. Iacoboni, "One way that I understand your pain is that in my own brain, I mimic what would happen to me if I felt the pain myself. And in females, the area that mimics the pain of others shows a bigger response. That's an indication that women's response is more empathic; they're feeling other people's pain more than the male participants are."

Dr. Christov-Moore confirmed that. "Our data suggest that females are better at feeling others' pain, at really getting the feeling that the other person is having right now. Female participants in the study showed relatively higher activation in a sensory area of the brain associated with pain than their male counterparts."

One British writer believes that, "You don't have to have spent five years monitoring people's yawns to know that it's nearly always the women, in social situations, who are alert to who's looking lonely, who hasn't spoken and who's in need of a crisp."

M.J.W. Loon of Utrecht University in Nederlands, offers another view on the reason why women outperform men on empathy. That reason, says the professor, "can be found in proximate mechanisms of empathy, like endocrine and neural differences between men and women. The masculine hormone testosterone is shown to inhibit empathy, while the feminine hormone oxytocin promotes empathic reactions to others."

In an Entrepreneur Magazine article about women leaders' reliance on empathy, Tracy Lawrence advises that though empathy is pigeonholed as a 'soft skill,' implying that it is warm, fuzzy, weak and unhelpful, it is in fact crucial for motivating others. The ability to motivate others is a requisite skill for leaders. In a Forbes Magazine article titled, *Empathy Is An Essential Leadership Skill -- And*

There's Nothing Soft About It, Prudy Gourguechon writes that the United States Army's Field Manual on Leader Development is one of the best resources on leadership that she has ever seen, and that it insists repeatedly that empathy is essential for competent leadership. Leaders of character display empathy, the manual advises. The capacity for empathy is an important attribute for leaders to possess it also says, and cautions leaders to learn more about the pitfalls associated with empathy failures.

Gourguechon writes that, "Empathy enables you to know if the people you're trying to reach are actually reached. It allows you to predict the effect your decisions and actions will have on core audiences and strategize accordingly. Without empathy, you can't build a team or nurture a new generation of leaders. You will not inspire followers or elicit loyalty. Empathy is essential in negotiations and sales.

"Like the practice of self-awareness," she goes on, "empathy involves scanning large sets of data, sorting out what's noise and what's essential information. Very successful business leaders are often extremely fast information processors. With my clients who do not "suffer fools gladly," I recommend taking a moment to deploy a bit of empathy."

"Don't confuse empathy with making people happy or being nice," she further advises, arguing also that. "Essentially, empathy is a neutral data-gathering tool that enables you to understand the human environment within which you are operating in business and therefore make better predictions, craft better tactics, inspire loyalty and communicate clearly."   The experts at Business Professional Women's (BPW) International point out that women have a tendency to encourage participation and collaboration when running an organization.

They also have the ability to work with a clear vision, and earn people's trust because of that. Unlike men, they rarely use threats to change behavior, instead focusing on motivating colleagues and improving performance.

A person must already be in touch with his/her own emotions and understand how to express them, in order to be able to attune oneself to other people's feelings, to be empathic. Both formal study and popular consensus have agreed that women are generally more expressive of and more in touch with their own emotions, are less embarrassed by them and therefore, suppress them much less than do men.

Of course, Professors Krewel and Karim remind us, there have been notable exceptions to the idea that female leaders are more compassionate, nurturing or nonviolent leaders. As U.S. Secretary of State, Hillary Clinton advocated for U.S. military involvement in conflicts in Libya and Syria. British Prime Minister Margaret Thatcher started a war while in office, and famously slashed government funding for Britain's social welfare services.

It bears remembering, however, that despite differences in "natural" traits, both men and women are socialised to perceive and, therefore, enact leadership in the same ways – in male ways – because leadership has for so long been entirely the territory of men, and therefore, the standard. Furthermore, women entering the world of work outside the home, are mostly entering spaces that are traditionally, culturally and historically male, which have been set up by and for men, and are peopled by men.

Very often they find themselves, therefore, having to operate 'as if they were men' in order to succeed. In her famous Tilbury Speech in 1588, Queen Elizabeth I of England said, "I know I have the body of a weak, feeble woman, but I have the heart and stomach of a king..."

Very slowly, the times they are a-changin', yet even today, women's leadership is still not commonplace, and women occupying or vying for positions of leadership are still very much judged, and mostly negatively, against the standards set so very long ago by men. By and large, women still are generally advised to show themselves to be "more like the men" where leadership is concerned, which roughly translates to: show them who's the boss, be tough, take charge, show yourself to be in command – and then are summarily faulted for both trying to be like men, as well as for failing to be like men!

One French study reported that, "Male perception of women leaders is changing, certain stereotypes are disappearing, and it is no longer "absolutely necessary for a woman to dress like a male CEO in order to gain recognition". But, women very often do indeed find it necessary to adopt traditional male leadership styles and behaviours in order to even be considered for entry into leadership, and then to stay in, if they do get admitted. Then they are punished for it.

Feminine leadership is said to be a 21st century model that's emerging out of the old, hierarchical, top-down, control model to focus on a well-rounded, healthier approach to business and community. In *The Power of Feminine Leadership* Tiffany Kelly tells us that, "Masculine is a focus on self and therefore, survival, and feminine is a focus on the other and the ability to thrive…Men who are taught that they have to be masculine are leading in a way that is focused on survival. Meaning that competition, the quest for power, divisiveness, and fear are being used...(and) lack true creativity and connectivity. Feminine leadership creates space in cultures for unique creativity, inclusiveness, collaboration and supportive competition."

Feminine leaders tend to have high emotional intelligence. Daniel Goleman published a book on emotional intelligence in which he posits that emotional intelligence is becoming "twice as important as cognitive ability in...distinguishing competencies."

Emotional intelligence has four parts, he says: self-awareness, self-management, social awareness, and relationship management. Teams led by people who possess high emotional intelligence tend to work hard and persevere through rough patches, he believes, and they also develop deeper bonds of trust, which are essential when, for example, employment statuses seem fragile.

"Right now, plenty of workers are dealing with tremendous fear," warns Ungerboeck, referring to the economic uncertainties of the COVID-19 pandemic. "Those guided by empathetic leaders will likely have an easier time working through their stresses, while others operating under a "business as usual" manager may become disengaged and resentful."

Tiffany Kelly believes that many people mistakenly assume that masculine and feminine leadership energies are gender specific, urges that people remember that both types of traits are present in both genders, and advises that we put our collective global efforts into empowering every person in a position of leadership to tap into both their feminine and masculine energies in a way that empowers everyone around them to do the same. "Make no mistake," she warns, "leaders will be judged by how they react during this historic moment.

In an article published in the Harvard Business Review, Bill George seems to be speaking of emotional intelligence and feminine leadership when he says that, "In the 21st century, the most successful leaders will focus on sustaining superior performance by...empowering leaders at all levels...and collaborating throughout the organization."

This is the approach taken by New York City fashion designer Eileen Fisher. She subscribes to a philosophy of "leading through listening" which she says has been integral to the success and longevity of her company. It is an unconventional leadership structure that "reflects Ms. Fisher's belief that consensus is more important than urgency, and that collaboration is more effective than hierarchy," wrote David Gelles in the New York Times. Recent research from Development Dimensions International, a global leadership consulting firm, reports that only about forty percent of leaders surveyed are proficient in this social skill – empathy. Taking the average of the women-in-leadership figures reported by Catalyst, the result is that only 44% of leadership in the workplace is female.

Feminine models of leadership are far from standard. In many cases, empathy is not necessarily considered a particularly useful or positive trait. Writing for Entrepreneur magazine, Krister Ungerboeck reminds us that difficult situations reveal why empathy is important in leadership, and that crises like the COVID-19 pandemic serve to drive the lesson home.

Prime Minister Jacinda Ardern of New Zealand is credited with having shown the world that feminine, that is to say, empathetic leadership isn't just acceptable – it is also a powerful force, and very helpful in times of trouble. Her response to the bombing of mosques in Christchurch, New Zealand in March 2019, that killed fifty people, moved Beth Daley of The Conversation to write that, "In the past, many women have felt the need to adopt traditionally masculine traits to succeed in the male-dominated world of politics. Ardern's willingness to embrace an openly female leadership style is a relatively new phenomenon."

WHEN WOMEN LEAD

113

MANY WOMEN IN LEADERSHIP
=
CLEARER COMMUNICATION

Ninety percent of leadership is the ability to communicate something people want.

\- Dianne Feinstein

Communication is the exchange of information. Communication is essential in all human interactions; it is vital to each and every successful relationship between and among humans. It would absolutely not be an overstatement to assert that communication is a life and death issue − how well one lives, indeed, whether one does live depends to an inestimable degree on the success of the interactions and relationships that one engages and encounters.

Relationships are built on communication. Relationships are more or less successful in direct proportion to the quality of communication between or among parties. One college textbook defines communication as the process of generating meaning by sending and receiving verbal and nonverbal symbols and signs that are influenced by multiple contexts. It further explains that every communication involves sender, message and recipient, and introduces the notion of noise and interference in the transferring of information. Under the word communication, some dictionaries will say that communication is the imparting or exchanging of information by speaking, writing or using some other medium.

Corporate and life-skills trainers coach that communication is simply the act of transferring information from one place, person or group to another, and that the quality of that act of transfer is oftentimes of greater import than the actual content of the communication. That is to say, it's not what you say, it's how you say it.

That communication is essential for survival is a principle that stands on its own; needs no qualifiers; is applicable to every species and to all interactions between and among them. Communication lies at the core of the very existence of all species that live on the earth. It has been found that even plants communicate, apparently. Biological scientists say they have found evidence that plants send messages to one another using "chemical languages" that are transmitted through the air, leaf to leaf, branch to branch and through networks of roots under the ground. These chemical communications support the growth and survival of plants. They help plants protect themselves from insects and pests, transmit information about other phenomena in nature such as the availability of water. Plants even communicate to one another about "trauma" such as cutting, harvesting and so on.

The most extensive, expansive and precise system of communication of all is thought to be that of the human species, and in that realm, scientists have identified four basic types of communication – verbal, non-verbal, written and visual. Verbal communication is the use of language to transfer information through speaking or sign language. Nonverbal communication is the use of body language, gestures and facial expressions to convey information to others. Written communication is information passed through symbols such as letters, numbers or pictures. Photographs, art, drawings, sketches, charts and graphs are all examples of visual communication.

Language, i.e. verbal and written communication among human beings, is structured in words and sentences, with other factors such as tone and inflection in delivery indicating and affecting meaning, interpretation and significance. Nonverbal cues in human communication accompany the verbal, can be both intentional and unintentional, and also affect reception and interpretation of the verbal communication. John Locke, a linguistics professor at Lehman College in New York, believes that speech and language could not have evolved before humans began living in large social groups.

Some theories posit that language was developed primarily by women in primitive societies. It is logical, the thinking goes, that women, interacting very intensely and for longer periods at a time with one another in the day-to-day routines of cultivating, gathering and preparing food, caring for children, the elderly, ill or injured and so on, would have of necessity, developed a complex and widely-applicable system of communication amongst themselves.

In 2001, researchers identified a gene to which they gave the name FOXP2, and its protein, which they suspect has played a role in the development of human language. That protein has since come to be called "the language protein" since "higher levels are found in the more communicative sex" of every species which has been tested so far.

In some birds, the males, which are more vocal and active in displaying to attract a mate, or lekking to project dominance and defend territory, have more of this protein, but in human beings, girls have more than boys. According to some researchers, women speak about three times as much as men. The Journal of Neuroscience does caution, however, that although sex differences in early language acquisition and development in children are well documented, and that on average, girls tend to speak earlier and with greater complexity than do boys of the same age, scientists continue to debate the origin and significance of these differences.

Yet, "Women talk a lot," is standard fare for comedians universally. "What do women talk about so much?" men wonder everywhere. "Women don't just talk; we communicate," is what women say, and that is a distinction of immense significance. In fact, communication and language researchers have found that women tend, more easily than men, to read between the lines and pick up emotional and social cues. Even as babies this tendency seems clear, they say – boy babies are attracted to spatial stimuli such as hanging and moving objects, while girl babies pay greater attention to social stimuli like faces and voices.

Research indicates that women are very effective listeners and are also more expressive than men. Women tend to truly listen to what other people have to say; they allow people to tell complete stories or to just vent, whereas men will immediately start looking for a response or a solution, and often interrupt the speaker to voice their perspective and advice. The upshot of this approach often is that they are effectively distracted from perceiving all that is being communicated, and consequently, they frequently miss the finer points of the communication. Their response can then sometimes seem off-topic or be unsatisfactory – to the more or less slight frustration of the women with whom they interact.

One axiom has it that women empathise and men systemise; that women communicate to connect, while men communicate to compete, because human beings are wired that way.

In great segments of the traditional world as constructed by men, the organizational structure has historically been hierarchical, with clear lines of command. The communication patterns that serve these types of relationships are very often direct and directive, short and to the point. In the military, in team sports, on job sites, in offices and governments, men typically, almost instinctively recognize and acknowledge a leader, give or receive instructions, follow directives and carry out tasks. Even in social interactions, the relationships and communications of men tend very much to hold to this order.

Generally-accepted definitions of leadership have required that leaders be people who naturally and instinctively fix things, provide solutions to problems, tell people what to do. Previously generally-accepted definitions of leadership, such as might be required in hunting and in war, for example, have taught men to do this, to communicate always in terms of "problem, solution, action". It is now being made clear, however, that truly effective leadership communication is about listening as much as it is about speaking. It requires knowledge of personality and attention to context. It understands that leading people is not only about problems to be fixed, or people to be told what to do, but rather that there are feelings, emotions and context to be considered.

In the realms of women, consensus, cooperation and sharing are foundational, and entail complex interaction and communication. Partly as a result, women's conversations on any matter will often tend to take more time from initiation to conclusion than those of men discussing the same subject. In either environment, however, clear communication is a core leadership function.

One workplace study in India had determined that every day, managers spend seventy to ninety percent of their time communicating with others. Clearly, successful and effective leadership in an environment such as this demands excellent communication skills. Having these skills makes it possible for the leader to handle the rapid flows of information, think with clarity, express ideas and share information with a multitude of audiences within the organization and on the outside – colleagues, customers, partners and other stakeholders, and influencers.

Researchers and experts conclude that since women listen well and are empathetic, they have a strong understanding of what drives people and can be very good at motivating groups and teams, since a good leader is able to inspire and motivate others, and doing so through communicating effectively. Furthermore, they say, women need not be concerned, despite the historical – or hysterical! – perplexity of men, for there is no such thing as overcommunication.

In the American Journal of Business Education, Priscilla Berry writes "No doubt about it…professional women who communicate effectively and confidently go further faster in their careers than those who do not. This most important of all skills (is) required to get your ideas across, resolve conflicts, shine in meetings, persuade and influence others, and rise in the ranks of any corporation…"

"While women certainly know how to talk – studies show that women tend to express themselves more eloquently than men – they're also great at listening and hearing the other side," writes business woman, Whitney English. "Listening is an all-too-often forgotten skill today, and many leaders use their positions of power primarily to tell others how to do things.

It's also important to note that communication is more than just talking. It's about perceiving body language and feelings – something that women tend to excel at. Since women have a strong understanding of what drives people, they're great at motivating their teams."

In an article entitled "Four Great Communicators and What They Taught Us", the Annenberg School for Journalism and Communication at the University of Southern California includes an observation of Oprah Winfrey. "Even if you are the sort who thinks that Oprah Winfrey is a tad on the annoying side," it reads, "you've got to admit that she does have a good handle on the whole communication thing.

Winfrey understands that listening is as important—if not more important—than speaking when it comes to communicating. She speaks out about issues that are on the minds of the people in her audience, and she does so honestly. People trust her because she comes off as genuinely interested in others. She built an entire empire like none before, out of her skills at communicating, both on screen and off."

Communication is the foundation of diplomacy, negotiation and compromise, all three being factors that contribute positively to good relations and the advancement of peace and development, and equality. Listening makes success possible in all three.

L.R. Robbins maintains that communication serves four major functions within a group or organisation, control, motivation, emotional expression and information, the most important being information, because every member of the organisation needs information with which to make decisions, experience and express emotions and be motivated, and to exercise control over themselves and their environment.

Angela Ahrendts made the move from CEO of Burberry, a British luxury brand where she built her reputation as a great communicator to being vice-president of retail and online stores at Apple. She is credited with having transformed Burberry from "a small company with a tarnished image" to one of the UK's greatest brands. She was included in an International Women's Day list celebrating Great Female Communicators compiled by Jago, a national and international communications and public relations practice headquartered in Belfast, Ireland. "She makes our list because she is a great listener. Angela listened to what consumers and the global market wanted from a company like Burberry and used this information to transform the business."

In summing up her strategy for political communicating, Rania Al Mashat, Egypt's Minister of International Cooperation says, "We are not just communicating with them, we are including them."

People use the information they get to help them identify and evaluate options and choices. With the competitive pressures facing organizations today, Robbins says, successful strategy formulation, decision making, motivating, team building, and negotiating depend on leaders' ability to communicate effectively. Siobhán Talbot, the Chief Executive of Ireland's biggest food group, Glanbia, is "arguably Ireland's most powerful and influential business woman," says Jago. She is known for her positivity, work ethic and communication skills...and is only the second woman to head a listed company in Ireland.

Suze Wilson, a researcher on leadership, says that the COVID-19 communication strategy of New Zealand's Prime Minister, Jacinda Ardern, "is pushing political communication 10 years forward – it is highly inclusive, empathetic...and breaks the barriers that exist between politicians and citizens by directly listening to their needs and challenges."

The Encyclopaedia Britannica says that Nina Simone "created urgent emotional intensity by singing songs of love, protest, and Black empowerment in a dramatic style, with a rough-edged voice."

In 2012, Virginia "Ginni" Rometty became president and CEO of IBM, the first woman to hold the top position in the company's 100-year history. According the Little Pink Book, people in the know say that although her business savvy did, of course, help her rise through the ranks, it was actually her communication skills that got her to the top. According to an IBM executive who's been in meetings with her, Rometty personally connects with everyone in the room with "incredible eye contact that makes you want to follow her lead."

"She communicates confidently, clearly and colorfully, all important traits when articulating a vision for the future success of her company and inspiring the people who will help accomplish that success." When Rometty announced her retirement from IBM at the beginning of 2020, after a forty-year career of sales and building up IBM's big technology services business, Frank Gens, chief analyst of IDC, a technology research firm, had this to say, "It's been her eight-year project to reposition the company, and after the positive report last quarter, she's declared victory and retired."

Hilton Als once said of the writing in one of Toni Morrison's books, "The brilliance of this conversation is in its economy and the reality of the women's talk."

"…my writing earns me trust," Arundhati Roy has said. "My real royalties, I feel, is this. The fact that I can go to places that are usually unwelcoming and, because of what I've written, be embraced and trusted and invited to stay for lunch."

Trust, above all, is what powers leadership. And trust is engendered and maintained through communication.

MANY WOMEN IN LEADERSHIP
=
STRONGER MEDIA

*The key to realizing a dream is to focus
not on success but on significance.*
— Oprah Winfrey

In pretty much any place around the world, when a conversation arises among or about media personalities – as in television, film, magazines, even news – one name that always comes up is, Oprah Winfrey.

Black and female, in the United States, and not "built to suit a fashion model's size", Oprah has anyhow designed an image and constructed a media empire that has reached around the world. Women in tiny rural villages and massive cosmopolitan cities know Oprah – have watched her, laughed with her, cried with her, lost and gained weight with her, celebrated and cheered with her. "Oprah's on!" was a message transmitted daily across streets and courtyards, down telephone lines and along shopping carts, from woman to woman, around the world for decades, literally. It was code and reminder for women to take a moment for themselves, share, experience, learn and get inspired.

In 2011, Oprah "retired" from her week-day talk show which she used to host in her Harpo Studios in Chicago. She now focuses on her OWN television network and some radio work, producing and appearing in a very select list of movies, and supporting and partnering with others in creating films, theatre and other storytelling art worth watching.

Since Oprah, there has been nothing like Oprah. But over the ages before Oprah, there were many women in many countries pushing against every barrier, every obstacle set up to deny women expression, contribution, inclusion and work, in media and elsewhere. These women were part of the workforce that dug the trenches and paved the road so that the phenomenon that was Oprah could materialise. Oprah herself has talked about the challenges she endured in her climb to the position she now occupies in the world of media. Her first job in media was a part-time stint reading news for a local radio station in Tennessee.

In 1928, Jamaican journalist, poet, and publisher Una Marson declared, "What man has done women may do." She became Jamaica's first woman editor and, still in her twenties, published her own magazine, The Cosmopolitan, which made her the first magazine publisher in her country. She went to London in 1932 and became the first black woman to be employed by the BBC, working for that entity during World War II.

In England, she was editor of *The Keys,* a newspaper promoting understanding between people of all colours, and campaigned against the "colour bar" that had prevented her from finding work when she first arrived in England. In 1941, she was hired by the BBC Empire Service onto a programme named *Calling the West Indies*, in which messages from World War II active-duty soldiers were read on the radio to their families in the islands. In 1942, she became the producer of the programme but was, eventually, forced out of that producer job by powerful white men.

In 1995, the Beijing Declaration had called on governments to address the "inequality in women's access to and participation in all communication systems, especially in the media." In 2009, a booklet for journalists prepared by UNESCO, reported that in many countries women are strongly represented in newsrooms, but media are still very male dominated when the top positions are examined.

"Strongly represented" in 2009 would have been considered an improvement on 1995, except that the same 2009 report also included the notice that "Women are marginalised in the news, both in the content of the jobs they do, and in the opportunities they have to make their way in the profession."

Women have, indeed, been present and active in radio, television and The Press almost from the very beginning. Women have been leading from in front and from behind. In fact, given the position they held, and to large degree still occupy in societies, women have been mostly leading from behind, but they have always been in the game. Women have never opted out. Success has been hard won. Advancement has been slow, but it has come, and in the process, it has elevated everyone.

In 1858, Bessie Rayner Parkes became the principal editor of the first feminist British periodical, The English Woman's Journal, and in 1860, she started the Victoria Printing Press. Constance Fulmer writes that the English Woman's Journal "was a very important part of the community and the women's right movement in England as it provided many women with employment, and an education that could never be taken away from them." In fact, when Parkes started the Victoria Printing Press, she did not know how to operate the machinery, so she paid a man to teach her, and then she trained her staff, which was entirely female throughout the existence of the enterprise.

Parkes was an activist for women's rights, and had a strong interest in the education of young women. Her circle of friends included writers and political activists in England, in other countries of Europe and in the United States. She was a part of the first group of women in England who began to formally agitate for women's right to vote.

Back when it was called "wireless, women were involved in radio. In keeping with women's place in society in that era, women were allowed to work only as telegraph operators, then as wireless operators. As the medium developed, however, and the societies began to change, women were radio amateurs, and some even built their own equipment from scratch.

In 1910, Mrs. M.J. Glass of San Jose, California, operated her radio as station FNFN. Gladys Kathleen Parkin was fifteen years old when, in 1916, she built her own radio and earned her first-class commercial radio operator's license. She worked with her brothers, John and Richard, in the family business which manufactured wireless instruments and operated a radio station in San Rafael, California.

In 1920, Eunice Randall became an engineer and announcer for the American Radio and Research Company (AMRAD) radio station, 1XE. In addition to her technical duties which included repairing equipment and "occasionally climbing the transmitting tower", she read children's stories and gave the police report over the air.

In Australia, Florence Violet Mackenzie founded the Women's Emergency Signaling Corps and trained thousands of service personnel in her signal instruction school.

In 1951, after the Second World War, Dutch feminist, economic historian and radio broadcaster Willemijn (Lilian) Hendrika, co-founded the International Association of Women in Radio, on the premise that radio could be used to bring women together across national boundaries to share ideas and information, and promote peace. It also eventually expanded its reach to include women working in television. The organization is now a global network with members from fifty-four countries, focusing on gender equality, and working to enhance the role of women in media and communications.

Today, a growing body of historical research is uncovering marginalized and often hidden histories of women in broadcasting and media generally, whose lives and work had been forgotten or ignored for many decades. Researchers are examining specific national contexts, from Argentina, Australia, Germany, Sweden, Turkey, the United Kingdom and the United States, for example, and have begun to write women and gender back into the history of broadcasting.

None of this exclusion and forgetting is new to women. Women's contributions have routinely been ignored, denied, appropriated and removed from history in just about every sector, in every era, but the reality is that women have, overall, played a very key role in the development of radio, both as broadcasters and as listeners. And women are still using radio as a medium for doing significant work in the world.

The UNESCO website tells that in September 2019, the BBC reported the story of Sediqa Sherzai who, in 2008, set up Radio Roshani, in the city of Kunduz in northern Afghanistan.

"Run by women and promoting women's rights, the station continues broadcasting today, in spite of death threats and other war-related challenges," says the BBC. "Its phone-in programmes provide an important space and public platform for women's voices and concerns. Radio Roshani is a powerful example of the strong relationship between women and radio today."

Writers on the subject attest that some programme formats and genres which we now take for granted, such as serials or soap operas, were conceived specifically for a female daytime radio audience. These types of programmes very intentionally targeted home-makers and stay-at-home moms who, at the time, were referred to as housewives. Soap operas were ongoing never-ending stories of people's everyday lives, dramatized to the nth degree, that were intended to satisfy the fantasies and assumed predilection for the melodramatic, of women, especially those who worked at home. The genres did much more.

The "feminine" slant of daytime radio, devised, decided and financed by men, had some significant and quite likely, unintended, consequences. It gave women a big say in shaping radio's general development and broadcasting practices. In 1997, in a book she titled, *Radio Voices: American Broadcasting*, Michele Hilmes, Professor of Media and Cultural Studies at the University of Wisconsin-Madison wrote that "under cover of daytime", radio serials addressed and confronted issues and concerns facing American women in the 1930s and 1940s.

With the advent of television, the woman-focused daytime programming became visual, and spawned another level of selling to women that now extended beyond soap and washing machines into fashion and cosmetics and other "feminine" lifestyle elements. Television was interactive in a way that radio never could be, and a kind of morphing occurred that was a blend of news programmes and interviews with public persons and personalities that became, eventually, a quite unique form of information and entertainment referred to as a talk show – a very particular kind of talk show.

Oprah Winfrey's career cycled from reading news on radio to reading news on television, but apparently, she failed to meet the threshold for objectivity and unfeeling required of reporters of hard news, so she was relieved of that assignment. In what was widely considered a demotion, she was offered the opportunity to co-host a television talk show. She accepted and the rest, as they say, is history.

Television as a form of media was first developed in the early part of the Twentieth century, and by mid-century was a fixture in much of the industrialised world, though its colours were only black-and-white. The visual nature of television provided interactivity and engagement that radio could not, but radio had reach with which television could not compete; for example, transistors and car radios make it possible for the audience to listen even while on the move, so radio continues to be a formidable medium for the dissemination of information and the improvement of communities, and women are still taking up leadership roles in the sector. The work that Sherzia is doing in Afghanistan serves as a perfect demonstration of the reach and power of radio.

Often when we speak of media, the first thing that comes to mind is news, and while, of course, news reporting is not by any means the extent, nor even the primary aspect of media, it is true that it has been through journalism and news reporting that many women have found an avenue through which they were able to enjoy a measure of personal expression, and lead some positive change in their communities and the world.

In her book, *Women Journalists and Feminism in China, 1898–1937*, Yuxin Ma examines how women journalists constructed Chinese feminism and debated patriarchy and women's roles in the newly-created public space of print media, at a time "when journalism became increasingly independent of and resistant to state control."

"A most remarkable change took place in the first half of the twentieth century in China," she writes. "Women journalists became powerful professionals who championed feminist interests, discussed national politics, and commented on current social events by editing independent periodicals. The rise of modern journalism in China provided literate women with a powerful institution that allowed them to articulate women's presence in the public space."

Oriana Fallaci died in 2006. She was an Italian journalist described variously as an agitator and a legend, because of an uncompromising vision of the world and a fierce interviewing style. While still a child, during the years surrounding the Second World War and Mussolini's regime, she had enlisted in the Italian Resistance alongside her father. A hatred of fascism and authoritarian regimes, engendered through these experiences in her childhood, remained strong throughout her life.

She was famous for her war-time reporting and her interviews with powerful personalities and international political figures of the time. One of her biographers wrote that, "To retrace Fallaci's life is to retrace the course of history from World War II to 9/11." It is said that, "occasionally, her interviews actually influenced history, or at the very least the pace and rhythm of events."

Ida B. Wells was born into enslavement in the United States, during the time of the American Civil War. After the emancipation proclamation, she found work in Tennessee as a teacher and then became co-owner and writer for the Memphis Free Speech and Headlight Newspaper, reporting on incidents of racial segregation and inequality. She was an investigative journalist and educator, an early leader in the civil rights movement. Although she was present in Niagara Falls for the founding of the National Association for the Advancement of Colored People (NAACP), her name is not mentioned as an official founder, says WomensHistory.org.

In the 1890s, Wells wrote articles and a pamphlet titled *Southern Horrors: Lynch Law in all its Phases,* that documented lynching in the southern United States. Her expose about an 1892 lynching enraged locals, who burned her press and drove her from Memphis. After a few months, her biography indicates, the threats became so bad she was forced to move to Chicago, Illinois.

In 1963, Gloria Steinem took a job working as a Playboy bunny so she could gather information, undercover, to write her seminal article, *A Bunny's Tale*. She co-founded Ms. magazine in 1971, with Dorothy Pitman Hughes because, she said, "There was really nothing for women to read, that was controlled by women." One edition of Ms. sold 300,000 copies in just eight days, when it published the names of women who had had abortions. The magazine made domestic violence a national issue when its August 1976 cover showed the bruised face of a battered woman

Steinem's biography, as it appears on the website of the Ms. Foundation for Women, says, "In 1973, Ms. Steinem joined with Patricia Carbine, Letty Cottin Pogrebin and Marlo Thomas to create the Ms. Foundation for Women...In 1968, she had helped to found New York magazine, where she was a political columnist and wrote feature articles. As a freelance writer, she was published in Esquire, The New York Times Magazine, and women's magazines as well as for publications in other countries. She has produced a documentary on child abuse for HBO, a feature film about the death penalty for Lifetime, and been the subject of profiles on Lifetime and Showtime."

The stated mission of the Coalition For Women In Journalism is to foster and support camaraderie among women journalists around the globe. The Coalition says, "We were the first to pioneer a worldwide support network for women journalists." The Coalition affirms that women journalists have changed the industry. "Today, with more women reporting and writing the news, audiences and readerships have greater access to stories. As a result, more diverse and dynamic coverage of the world is possible."

Despite organisations such as the Coalition for Women in Journalism, gratifying work in media is still not available to women in many parts of the world. Restrictions on women's autonomy, freedom to travel or engage the profession they choose, and limited information and media infrastructure, often combine with cultural norms to deny women work as journalists and reporters, and as radio or television professionals. Those restrictions might be impeding many, but they are certainly not stopping women from pushing through and occupying leading positions at every level, and that will, eventually, result in greater inclusion of women. Women around the world are working to bring that about.

There is a fast-expanding network of African women journalists, called WanaData Africa, on a mission to change the digital media landscape of the continent by engaging data-driven projects that elevate female voices and shed light on under-reported stories. They say they are redefining the careers of members, are refashioning them into "newsroom innovators". On the network's website is written: The network recently launched Trafficking Africa, a transnational reporting project that will explore the national and international dimensions of human trafficking. Other cross-border projects include BornPerfect, which highlights stories of those affected by female genital mutilation, and

GenderGap, a project that focuses on gender inequality in income, property rights and education.

Media is defined as the main means of mass communication – broadcasting, publishing, and the internet – regarded collectively. Around the world and across the ages, examples abound of women who took to the media available to them to advance learning, to engage discussion, and to inform about politics, social issues, science, art, fashion and more. Some, such as Enheduanna of Sumeria, thought to be the first named author in world history, were writers of poetry. Others, like Jane Austen of England or Chimamanda Ngozi Adichie of Nigeria, have chosen to publish novels.

Many have been journalists, traveling the world to investigate the lives, cultures and histories of others; to gather information that would stimulate thought and engender action; and to enlighten and enhance people's perceptions and purviews. These women make their contributions across various media in myriad sectors – newspapers, magazines, television, radio, film, the internet – women with names familiar to people in many parts of the world: Oriana Fallaci, Christiane Amanpour, Charlayne Hunter-Gault, Marie Colvin, Amy Goodman, Opra Winfrey, Barbara Walters, Carine Roitfeld, Jill Abramson, Joy Bramble, Tina Brown, Rose Willock, Jacqueline Charles, Arianna Huffington, Zahra Hankir and Zeinab Badawi, to name just a very few.

The reality is that there are very few women in the top ranks of leadership in media companies of any kind and, notes Jeremy Barr, in Advertising Age magazine,

"Some executives worry that the imbalance is bad…for their products and their businesses as a whole."

"The more women CEOs there are, the more women CEOs there will be," was the response, reportedly, of Vivian Schiller, who served as the first female of the US National Public Radio from 2009 to 2011, says Michele Weldon, in an article entitled *Why More Women Leadership In Media Would Change The Stories of The World.*

The Alliance for Women in Media reports that representation of women in America's newsrooms is about "one third of newsroom employees overall, with a higher number employed at online-only sites than at newspapers," according to the 2016 Diversity Survey from the American Society of News Editors. Some women leading in media today are influencers in social networking spaces; they are bloggers, vloggers and the like, exploiting modern technological opportunities in ways that change the landscape of our collective lives.

The OECD reports that social media has proved to be a powerful vehicle for bringing women's rights issues to the attention of a wider public, galvanising action on the streets of cities around the world, and encouraging policymakers to step up commitments to gender equality. But also that while, globally, women are greater users of social media than men (McPherson, 2014), many women, especially in developing countries, still do not have access to this technology due to infrastructure, costs and discriminatory social norms. But, women find ways.

The ways in which women communicate and the purposes for which they connect are evident right across the social media space. There is a preponderance of women's groups which all declare their reason for existing as some form of connecting. Women start these groups, many of them with memberships grown into the tens and hundreds of thousands, so that they can share stories, make connections and stay in touch with family or friends. "Specifically," say Krasnova, Veltri, Nicole and Bauxmann in the Journal of Strategic Information Systems, "while women are mainly driven by relational uses, such as maintaining close ties and getting access to social information on close and distant networks, men base their continuance intentions on their ability to gain information of a general nature."

On the blog, Feminism In India, Jyoti Ahlawat writes about *How Social Media Has Become A Site For Sisterhood In the COVID-19 Pandemic*. "Do social media platforms like Facebook, Twitter or Instagram to name a few of the many, have the capacity to transform into an anchor for women," she asks, "a free virtual space for women to connect, create and share their posts imbued with wit, humour and emotions which resonate with one and all?"

"The answer, undoubtedly, is a yes," she affirms. "The online media have brought out the spirit of solidarity and unity among women…"

Lebanese-British journalist Zahra Hankir has published a collection of essays by Arab women journalists who have worked in the Middle East and North Africa. The goal of *Our Women on the Ground:*

Essays by Arab Women Reporting from the Arab World, she says was to bring attention to "underreported tales and the women who tell them." In that book, Hannah Allam describes how, in 2004, at the time of the American invasion of Iraq, during a siege that dragged on for weeks, she had hidden with women inside a Shiite Muslim mosque in Najaf. She tells how, when she and her translator did finally escape, they were saved by two Iraqi women who drove them back to their hotel.

Recounting her time spent with the women, and describing relationships forged and insights acquired therein, Allam wrote, "Every time Iraq began to unravel, it was women who worked the hardest to stitch it back together."

MANY WOMEN IN LEADERSHIP
=
HIGHER EDUCATION

The question isn't who's going to let me;
it's who is going to stop me.
- Ayn Rand

If you educate a man you educate an individual, but if you educate a woman you educate a nation, is said to be an African aphorism. This axiom is printed in the very first pages of a commemorative book published by buildOn, an organisation whose mission is, in part, to break the cycle of poverty, illiteracy, and low expectations through service and education, and to change the world by building schools in some of the economically poorest countries on the planet.

In that same book is written the story of a young woman from Nepal named Sonu. The story describes some aspects of the difficult life that Sonu has lived. It recounts how she almost got sold to human traffickers and then came close to being murdered by the same person who had tricked her with promises of marriage in India, when he found he had been foiled in his attempt to sell her.

Sonu is a Dalit, which means she is of the caste referred to, in India, as *"untouchable"*. In classical Sanskrit, *dalit* meant broken or scattered, and is a term that has also been applied to 'the working people, the landless and poor peasants, women and all those who are being exploited politically and economically, and in the name of religion'.

Sonu does not know her precise age. She had never been to school but had worked as a child labourer doing domestic work from the age of about nine. She was illiterate. Of the several languages spoken in the mountain region where she lived, she was unable to speak any single one properly. Her verbal communication was a mixture of Nepali, Hindi and one of the local mountain languages. Her lack of education and language made it difficult for her to think critically and use reason to arrive at decisions.

With her limited reasoning abilities, then, Sonu had accepted what she had thought was an honest offer of marriage from a man who had come to her village saying he was looking for a wife. She had agreed to go to India with him and be married there. Before they reached the border with India, however, they were intercepted by an organization working against human trafficking, and she was freed by them. Unable to get back to her village of origin, she eventually made her way back to a village in the Nepalese mountains and it was there that she came into contact with buildOn.

The adult literacy programmes offered by buildOn teach women like Sonu to read and write, and how to start small businesses. Sonu took one of buildOn's adult literacy programmes and helped in the construction of a school building in the village. She is now one of the women whose personal empowerment has changed their own lives, the lives of their children, and of their village as a whole.

As is reported by many other organisations working all around the world with missions similar to buildOn, this new knowledge, this new capability and competence, engenders a level of self-confidence that helps the women gain some independence and begin to have some control over their own lives. They then educate their daughters, so there arises a new generation of women who are better equipped to avoid the traditional deep dependency and the kinds of dangerous situations that can so often come with poverty and illiteracy, such as had happened with Sonu.

On the basis of the education they receive, these newly-educated women gain increased confidence in their abilities and their sense of having value and worth, despite the deprived conditions in which they live. They become aware of their ability to truly improve life for their families and communities. They often become a driving force in the development of their villages, in subtle and other more visible ways, and contribute ever greater value to the wider communities.

"There is no tool more effective for development than the empowerment of women," the seventh United Nations Secretary General of the United Nations, Kofi Annan, had said.

"Education is the most powerful tool countries have for boosting economic growth, increasing prosperity and forging more just, peaceful and equitable societies. Where educational deprivation exists, it breeds conflict and enables repression," says Wendy Kopp, the CEO and co-founder of Teach for All.

Education helps provide a woman with empowerment and a sense of self-worth. Women are the backbone of the communities, so nurturing and accommodating women's sense of personal value is critical to development and progress. "By 2050," writes Graca Machel, chair of the International Board of Trustees, African Child Policy Forum (ACPF) in The Guardian, "Africa will be home to around half a billion girls and young women. If respected and treated as equals, they have the potential to transform the continent's security and prosperity. This matters because every penny invested in girls' education, healthcare and social protection benefits society many times over, while failure to invest in girls results in monumental socioeconomic losses."

Ruth is a woman from Burkina Faso, mother of eight children, who had never attended school and could not read, or write her name. Every day, she rose before dawn to carry water, feed the animals and prepare breakfast for her extended family. Then, for a time, she went after that, to the worksite where a school was being built in her village, making repeated trips to fill cans of water for mixing cement, carting them back and forth on her head. Ruth said she did this to make sure that her daughters would have choices in their lives because she hoped education would bring a better future for her family. Today, her daughters are learning to read and write, and are empowered to marry later, get better jobs, healthcare, freedom from violence and more.

An educated female population increases a country's productivity and fuels economic growth, says the United Kingdom's Department for International Development, DfID. Educated girls can make informed choices - and from a far better range of options. Educating girls saves lives and builds stronger families, communities and economies. Some countries lose more than $1 billion a year by failing to educate girls to the same level as boys, DfID estimates.

In 2009, President Obama told an audience at Cairo University, Egypt, that "it is no coincidence that countries where women are well educated are far more likely to be prosperous..."

The contribution of women to a society's transition from pre-literate to literate is undeniable, say other workers in development. Basic education is key to a nation's ability to develop and achieve sustainability targets. Research has shown that education enhances the status of girls and women, improves agricultural productivity, enhances environmental protection and raises the standard of living, and *it is the mother in the family, i.e. a woman in the family, who most often urges children of both genders to attend – and who makes it possible for them to stay in school.*

In the early days of the United States of America, public schools did not exist and women were not allowed into universities. Girls were taught not much more than how to cook and sew. So, some intrepid women started schools for girls which came to be called "dame" schools. Other women established Sunday Schools, Sabbath Schools, kindergartens and the forerunners of today's public schools.

History books and *Her Story: A Timeline of the Women Who Changed America*, written by Jill S. Tietjen, PE and Charlotte S. Waisman, Ph.D, tell that in 1831, a woman named Prudence Crandall opened a school for the daughters of wealthy farmers in Canterbury, Connecticut, but when she admitted Sarah Harris, an African-American woman who wished to become a teacher, the parents of her other students were outraged and withdrew their daughters. Prudence closed the school and recruited free black students from New York, Philadelphia and Boston, in order to reopen her school for "young misses of colour".

The State of Connecticut, therefore, passed a law making it illegal to educate AfricanAmerican students from out of state, and Crandall was arrested, put on trial twice and convicted. She appealed and won. Her conviction was overturned but the townspeople were upset at her victory and set her school building on fire, broke windows, and made it altogether too difficult and unsafe for her to continue operating her school, so she left the state. She kept up her activism, however, by becoming involved in the women's suffrage movement and running a school in LaSalle County, Illinois.

In 1886, subsequent to strong lobbying from a small group that included the illustrious Mark Twain, a resident of Hartford, the Connecticut legislature passed a resolution honouring Crandall for her courage and moral strength, and awarded her a pension. In 1995, more than one hundred years after her death, she was named Connecticut's State Heroine. On the campus of Howard University, in Washington, DC, one of the country's Historical Black Colleges and Universities, in the Harriet Tubman quadrangle, is Crandall Hall, a residence hall, named in her honour.

Myrtilla Miner was an abolitionist who believed that education was the key to ending the institution of slavery in America. She taught in Rhode Island and Mississippi for a while, then in 1851, opened a school for African-American girls in Washington, DC. In 1853, she found a permanent home for what she called the Normal School for Colored Girls. Before the Civil War, hers was the only school that offered education beyond the elementary level for African-American girls, and she endured constant harassment even from city leaders. One of her students described her as "one of the bravest women I have ever known." The University of the District of Columbia traces its history back to Miner's Normal School. Today, an elementary school in the District of Columbia is named in her honour.

Elizabeth Peabody opened the first English-language kindergarten in the U.S. in Boston, Massachusetts in 1860. Peabody was a teacher and a writer who owned a bookstore where Margaret Fuller starting holding her "Conversations" in 1839, so women could engage in conversations on diverse topics.

"If you evaluate all the countries where poverty, hopelessness and violence abound, you will find that women are absent from the public square," says Jodi Shelton, founder of Shelton Group in Texas, USA. "The educated woman is a powerful force for good in the society." She is also considered a serious threat to the systems and institutions of the patriarchy, and in many countries meets with fierce, even homicidal, opposition.

Malala Yousefzai was born in Mingora, in the Swart Valley of Pakistan on July 12, 1997. As a young girl of 11, the Pakistani student used to write an anonymous diary for the BBC about what life was like under the harsh rule of the Taliban, in north-west Pakistan. The Taliban had forced schools to close and prohibited the education of girls. Malala's father ran a school for girls that the Taliban had ordered him to close. He refused. The Taliban threatened to kill both him and his daughter.

In October 2012, on her way home from school one day, a masked gunman boarded her school bus and asked, "Who is Malala?" and shot her in the head. Two of her friends were injured, also. Fortuitously, Malala and her two friends recovered and Malala continues to speak out in support of the education of girls.

Graça Machel, who has the singular distinction of having been the First Lady of Mozambique and later, of South Africa, was absolutely correct in her observation that, "When we invest in women and girls, we invest in the people who invest in everyone else."

Born Graça Simbine in what was then called Portuguese East Africa, Graça grew up without a father. He had made his living and provided for his family by farming and working in the mines of South Africa, but died just weeks before his daughter was born. The family legend has it that he made his wife promise that their unborn child would have proper schooling, and Graça's mother kept her word. "We were a poor family," Machel has said, "but I had the best education."

Young Graça Simbine got a scholarship to high school in Maputo, the capital of Mozambique. She was the only African in the class with forty white students. She asked herself, "Why is it that I'm made to feel strange in my own country? They're the foreigners, not me. Something is wrong here."

Later, she became an African freedom fighter with a mission to liberate and educate her people. After some time spent in Portugal, Graça joined FRELIMO, the Front for the Liberation of Mozambique, as a courier. She later was trained as a guerrilla fighter, and met and eventually married Samora Machel, the leader of the movement. When he became President of Mozambique in 1975, she became the minister of culture and education. "Graça Machel now showed her true colours," wrote Robert McClum, in England's The Guardian.

Within two years, she had boosted school attendance and lowered illiteracy in Mozambique. The number of students enrolled in primary and secondary schools rose from about forty percent of all school-aged children to over ninety percent for boys and seventy-five percent for girls.

Of the current African situation, Graça Machel says, "New research from the African Child Policy Forum shows that far too often, to be a girl in Africa means being denied education; getting married too young; sexual and emotional abuse at home and school; being barred from inheriting property; and being last in the queue when it comes to state spending on health, education and social protection.

"We urgently have to break the cycle of gender-based discrimination and inequality. Girls are key drivers of transformation, and investing in them will trigger a chain reaction that ultimately leads towards a peaceful and prosperous Africa. Investment in education should rise to at least 4% of GDP."

For years now, women in the US have been outnumbering men in rates of enrollment and graduation from tertiary education institutions. Citing the National Center for Education Statistics (NCES), Inc. magazine reports that, "Black women are the most educated demographic in the U.S. when you look at the number of associate and bachelor's degrees earned."

The NCES reports that between academic years 2000–01 and 2015–16, shares of bachelor's degrees earned by female students were 64 percent for Black students, 61 percent for American Indian/Alaska Native students, 60 percent for Hispanic students, 59 percent for students of two or more races, 56 percent for White students, and 54 percent for Asian/Pacific Islander students.

This has not, however, translated into higher earnings or higher positions at work for Black women in the professions. But, Black women are flocking to entrepreneurship, commercial activity that, by some measures, correlates highly to increases in personal and family wealth. From 2007 to 2018, the number of businesses owned by Black women grew by 164%, very nearly tripling in those eleven years.

Research conducted by Vincenzo Quadrini of Duke University seems to verify that correlation. He found that in the lower social classes, the percentage of families moving to a higher class is greater for workers who acquire a business than for those who continue to work for others. In the middle class, the percentage of families that are upwardly-mobile is higher than the percentage of downwardly-mobile families for the sub-sample of workers that become entrepreneurs, while the reverse is observed for those who remain employees of others.

That Black women in the United States are becoming more and more highly-educated and are contemporaneously choosing entrepreneurship over work in the employ of others to such greater degree than before, lends itself well to some very interesting and promising possibilities with respect to wealth and women's leadership in general.

For several decades, the increase in female enrolment in tertiary education in the University of the West Indies (UWI) also has outpaced that of males. For the first 35 years of its existence, beginning in 1948, UWI enrolled and graduated more men than women. That position was reversed in the 1982-83 academic year, writes the Jamaica Gleaner, and since then, the world-renowned university has seen an increasing number of female students being enrolled and graduating from the various programmes it offers at its campuses in Mona, Jamaica, St Augustine, Trinidad and Tobago, and Cave Hill, Barbados. In 2017, almost 70 per cent of the UWI enrolment were women.

Sarah Owen, Continuing and Professional Education Centre Director at The University of the West Indies Open Campus, says there is an obvious disparity in enrolment at the UWI when it comes to males and females. "So…the other thing we need to consider…we have a very restricted way of viewing education because when we hear education we think of formal schooling. So, we think of preschool, primary school, secondary school, university, but the root word for education," she says, "is "educere" which some would look at as simply meaning to lead forth." But, she also asks, "If what we are doing is not leading people forth, then are we actually engaged in education?"

What Owen is alluding to is the concept of education as being much broader than the solely academic. That perspective sees education as a learning process that goes way beyond what takes places within the walls of the classroom. Opportunities to learn are thought to present themselves outside of the traditional and formal teaching and learning environments, and are infinite in scope and in subject.

So, even while cleaving to the formal definition of education as "a process of acquiring knowledge through study, or imparting the knowledge by way of instructions or some other practical procedure", educators these days recognise three types of education processes: formal, informal and non-formal, all of which are impacted and supported greatly by information and telecommunications technologies. Information technology has become central to every form of education, for the ease of access it allows to the very broadest spectrum of knowledge and the greatest numbers of people. The industry which has sprung up to design, administer and manage cyberspace is overwhelmingly populated by men.

Currently, women's leadership is almost unnoticeable in the IT, telecommunications and cyberspace, although women use the internet about as much as men, although quite differently.

"Let's face it," writes Sam Daley for BuiltIn, "tech *still* has an issue with gender diversity…the five largest tech companies on the planet (Amazon, Apple, Facebook, Google and Microsoft) only have a workforce of about 34.4% women." Daley notes, in addition, that gender diversity breeds higher quality products, companies and sectors. Different backgrounds, experiences and ideas ultimately help make any business or industry stronger.

"The Internet has the power to drive economic growth and expand social opportunities," writes Carlos Iglesias, Senior Research manager at Web Foundation. "It has empowered people and changed the way we communicate with each other, opening up new worlds and new ways of thinking."

He also says that almost half the world is still offline, and the majority of those offline are women in developing countries. To be offline today means to miss out on learning and earning, accessing valuable services, and participating in the democratic public debate, raising concerns for gender equality and women's ability to contribute to development and progress, the reduction of poverty and so on.

In Africa, writes Ian Semple, Science writer at The Guardian, mobile phones drive the growth in internet access, but nowhere is it more expensive to be online…10 times more, as a proportion of income, than a typical OECD citizen pays. It is not surprising, therefore, that African women were the demographic who accessed the internet the least in the world, in 2017.

A 2012 article in the magazine The Atlantic titled, *How Cell Phones Are Bringing Rural Africans Into The Modern Economy*, was very optimistic when it stated that, "In Africa in particular, mobile payments have really taken off." This optimism corresponded with, and was part of the general hopefulness engendered by the stories being told of African market women and huskers using cell-phones to do business with one another and their clients, customers and counterparts, connecting the millions of women doing business on the outskirts of the formal structure economy in rural and urban areas.

In one survey conducted by the Web Foundation, a common remark from women in ten developing countries was that going online was simply not worthwhile. There are other forces at work, militating against women's inclusion. This continuing difficulty for women, has its roots in sexism and the patriarchy. In these societies, technology, and the wider online world, are seen as male preserves. Women access is limited in the same ways and with the same reasonings, in this as in any other sector of human living. A September 2020, article in Vox, tells this story.

"In a rural village in Kenya, a woman sets out to do her food shopping for the day. She needs cash before she heads to the market, but the nearest bank would be several days' walk. Instead, she takes out her phone and texts a password and a request for money. A few minutes later, she meets a man with a cell-phone and receives cash from him — the withdrawal that she made on her phone. She heads off, ready to do her errands." This encounter speaks equally of possibility and limitation.

In those countries where men and women are equally likely to go to university, or where women make up the majority of the university population, the digital gender gap is erased or reversed. In Jamaica, for example, more women are online than men – a reflection perhaps, says Semple, of the long-standing dominance of women at the University of the West Indies in Kingston.

As a result of the isolation, lockdown and social distancing forced upon the entire world in the wake of the COVID-19 pandemic, cyberspace has become the markets, streets, schools, offices and even concert halls, sports arenas and high fashion runways of the world. Access to the internet has progressed from being an important asset and medium of interaction to being an absolutely critical necessity, and access akin to a right.

Simultaneously, its weak spots and vulnerabilities have been more dangerously exposed and those dangers exacerbated proportionately. As in the physical world, the groups placed most at risk with regard to these dangers are women and children. Quick and robust responses are demanded. As in the physical world, the urgency of providing those responses will resonate more strongly with women.

The preponderance of evidence available from all sectors suggests that in this, as in all other spheres, the increased engagement of women will facilitate, if not entirely ensure, the quality and range of improvement necessary to make this new reality work best for all. It would help information technology serve everyone better. It would also ensure further narrowing of the gap between the education of girls and that of boys, a win-win from any and every quantitative calculation and qualitative perspective.

MANY WOMEN IN LEADERSHIP
=
GREATER WEALTH

I didn't learn to be quiet when I had an opinion.
The reason they knew who I was is
because I told them.
-    Ursula Burns

Money is important. Money is critical. It is foundational to economies – personal, national and global. Human societies have utilised the concept of money for millennia, in a variety of forms and always for the same reason – to ease and facilitate commercial activity.

Money is currency, is a universally-accepted medium of exchange for the goods and services we desire and need, and it had taken the form of paper or coins and increasingly, little cards made of plastic. Now, money is changing form again, becoming more and more bits and bytes in an intangible, invisible and – largely incomprehensible to many – online financial realm. Money is important for individuals and families as much as for countries and governments, and for non-profit organisations as much as for commercial enterprises. Generally speaking, the more money one has relevant to the amount that one needs, the more comfortable is the life one leads.

We refer to money earned as income or revenue depending on the sector in which we are operating, but they really are one and the same thing. Income or revenue is what comes to us when we sell our goods or services to others. And, generally speaking, the more there is of that coming to us in the transaction, the better we feel.

Using data from Credit Suisse, Oxfam has determined that the richest sixty-two people in the world, one percent of the global population, have as much wealth among them as does the poorest half of the population of the entire world. 62 people, therefore, own property having a monetary value equivalent to the combined property of hundreds of millions of people. The irony is that at both ends of this scale, women stand out for comprising the lower proportion of the very richest and the higher proportion of the very poorest.

In the countries of the world, millions of people live in poverty, even dire, deadly poverty, and engage in activities of all sorts, legal and not, even dangerous and life-threatening, in seeking to remedy their living conditions, which are subject to their ability to have access to money. The group which is at most risk and which suffers most, across the board, without question, is women.

The tax codes of many countries still list "head of household" and in most households, the "head" is a man. Often that person is the only person earning an income outside of the home, and in many cases, it is barely enough to keep the family satisfactorily housed and fed. Sometimes, it is not adequate even for that. In some countries and communities, women are either not permitted, or are actively discouraged from working outside the home, which often means they have no access to money of their own, and therefore no agency or independence.

When women receive income, however, whether "unearned income" i.e. as returns from investments, pensions, inheritances and such, or earn payment for work conducted at the home or out in the world, a family's conditions tend to improve. Women's earnings are a boost to household income and it is a very well-established fact that women spend their income different to men. Women everywhere spend more of their money on children and for the home than do men, research indicates.

WomenDeliver, which describes itself as a leading global advocate championing gender equality and the health and rights of girls and women, finds that girls and women spend up to ninety percent of their earned income on their families, while men spend only about thirty or forty percent. Measures such as child-survival probabilities increase up to twenty times in some regions of the world, when unearned income accrues to women rather than to men.

World Bank evidence from countries as varied as Brazil, China, India, South Africa, and the United Kingdom, shows that when women control more household income – either through their own earnings or through cash transfers – children benefit as a result of there being more spending on food and education. And, we have already seen the many instances that show how women use their resources to become developers of human capital for their communities.

In 2006, Professor Muhammad Yunus of Bangladesh was awarded the Nobel Peace Prize in recognition of his work in poverty alleviation and the empowerment of poor women. In explaining his bank's decision to prioritize women when making micro-loans to the poor without financial security, Yunus said, "For women to be granted the loan has a definite effect on the family. There is no need to do more research on that today.

Children benefit automatically, with better clothes and food. We can see the situation changing. Men often spend the money on themselves; women spend it on the family. The bank's practice has meant a social revolution in Bangladesh."

In a Forbes Magazine article titled, *"The Results Are In: Women Are Great For Business, But Still Getting Pushed Out"*, Janet Burns reported on a University of California, Davis Graduate School of Management study which revealed that "big California companies with at least some women at the top, performed considerably better than ones with mostly male boards and executives."

The top twenty-five most gender-diverse companies in California have shown a median return on assets and equity that are at least seventy-four percent higher than for the entire sample of four hundred publicly-owned companies examined in the study. The Peterson Institute for International Economics did a survey of twenty-two thousand firms from ninety-one countries and found that, a profitable firm at which thirty percent of leaders are women, could expect to add more than 1 percentage point to its net margin compared with an otherwise similar firm with no female leaders. By way of comparison, the typical profitable firm in one sample had a net profit margin of 6.4 percent, so one-percentage point increase represents a 15 percent boost to profitability.

Joe Carella, the assistant dean at the University of Arizona Eller College of Management, told CNBC, "We found that companies that have women in top management roles experience what we call 'innovation intensity' and produce more patents – by an average of 20 percent more than teams with male leaders." In an article bearing the title *Companies with more female executives make more money: here's why,* CNBC reporting asserts that a large female presence is also associated with higher status. According to the Gender Forward Pioneer (GFP) Index, the "most admired" companies have twice as many women at the senior management level as do less reputable companies. The GFP Index measures the percentage of the world's 500 largest companies, by revenue, with gender balance in their senior management teams.

Petersen Institute findings indicate that a strong female presence benefits the workplace environment in many ways. Having senior leaders who are female, creates less gender discrimination in recruitment, promotion and retention, a factor which gives a company a better chance of hiring and keeping the most qualified people. Carella tells about having been called in to help lower the high turnover rate of both male and female employees at a large U.S. tech company. His solution, he says, was to promote two senior female executives to positions where they could influence what had formerly been a boardroom run exclusively by men. The move ended up making the whole company more transparent, and employee retention increased; they stopped leaving at such a high rate.

These findings are corroborated by Catalyst Inc. whose work includes promoting the advancement of women into executive roles. Looking at financial results such as return on equity, return on sales and return on invested capital at the 500 largest U.S. corporations, they deduced that those with at least three women directors had notably stronger financial performance, on average.

In return on equity, on average, companies with the highest percentages of women board members outperformed those with the least by fifty-three percent, and in return on sales, the companies with more women board directors outperformed by 42 percent on average. In the area of return on invested capital, that lead was sixty-six percent, Catalyst found. When Fortune magazine published its 2019 edition of the annual list of the Most Powerful Women in the world of business, this was its opening paragraph: You still have to squint to spot the women leading large global businesses. In 2019, female executives were at the head of just fourteen of the world's 500 largest companies – and that was actually an improvement over the previous year, when there were only twelve. But zooming out – as *Fortune* does each year with this list – at women in powerful jobs across the international landscape i.e. outside the U.S., there's reason to think there's bigger change afoot.

The women on the list come from nineteen countries representing every continent except Antarctica. Many of them work for multinational firms in industries in which there have rarely been women at the top – industries such as chemicals, oil and gas, and metal manufacturing. Among these women are Jessica Tan of China's Ping An - insurance, banking, and financial services; Ilham Kadri of Solvay in Belgium which describes itself as a global leader in materials, solutions and chemicals; and Emma FitzGerald at Puma Energy whose headquarters are in Singapore. There are also Andrea Marques de Almeida who was promoted to Chief Financial Officer at Brazil's Petrobras, Anne Rigail, CEO at Air France and Maki Akaida, CEO of Uniqlo in Japan.

While they were early into their new, more powerful roles, Fortune said, and were still largely untested, what's significant is that they're in a position to make a difference – for their companies, for women and for the world in general. With women now representing 40 percent of the global labor force and more than half the world's university students, writes the International Monetary Fund (IMF), overall productivity will increase if women's skills and talents are used more fully. For example, if women farmers have the same access to productive resources such as land and fertilizers as do men, agricultural output in developing countries could increase by as much as 2.5 to 4 percent, according to the Food and Agriculture Organisation (FAO) of the United Nations.

Eliminating barriers against women working in certain sectors or occupations could increase output by raising women's participation and labor productivity by as much as 25 percent in some countries through better allocation of women's skills and talent.

Dozens of countries could see a 15% increase of GDP per capita if workforce gender gaps were closed, according to Word Bank studies. In the Middle East this number could be as high as 30%. Many studies have been completed which show how closing the gender gap actually results in raising a country's GDP. Gender equality, they find, is "smart economics". It can enhance economic efficiency.

Gender equality matters in its own right, however, and not only inasmuch as it can contribute to the bottom line of a company or country. Reports from a long list of organisations that include the IMF, the World Bank, the World Economic Forum and UN Women suggest that gender equality is important for and results in improvements to all sectors of societies, in the private and public spaces. Of course, equality in general, eases the pathways for equality in the occupation of positions of leadership.

For almost the entirety of recorded history, societies have insisted on and clung to gendered roles in homes and communities. Because of this, women leaders have been very few and far between although, there have been, of course, the occasional monarch, head of the family business, civic icon or head of government. The situation has begun to see some change in many parts of the world, however, but has altogether defied advancement in just as many others.

A recent study has examined the situation in France, for instance, and found that although things have changed drastically since the milestone date and epoch of 1968, and that there exist certain aspects that are peculiar to French culture, "no evidence has been found to suggest that France is in any way a "cultural exception" when it comes to issues of women's leadership and equality, in any sector . In other words, "The glass ceiling is still in place in French organizations, although a number of respondents deemed that this phenomenon is decreasing. There are still very few women at board level and they are often "relegated to positions in HRM (human resource management) and Communication".

Respondents said believe that the barriers of "male nepotism and co-opting" are factors that represent major obstacles in women's climb to the top of the corporate ladder and that gender diversity in France should be seen for its potential to be "an opportunity and a driving force in terms of innovation and attaining higher performance levels".

Researchers found a general consensus that women were often "stronger in the fields of organizational ability, anticipation, multi-tasking, and the general propensity to put their team's welfare before considerations of personal ambition". The researchers also reported that the majority of respondents in this study saw women-led corporations as being more successful, explaining that they believe that women "tend to be more effective in the field of financial management" as one example. Studies conducted all across the world bear this out.

In May, 2019, the International Labour Organisation (ILO) published an article with the heading *Women in leadership bring better business performance.* A new report, the article says, shows gender diversity improves business outcomes, and makes it easier to attract talent. It goes on to say that businesses with genuine gender diversity, particularly at senior levels, perform better, including seeing significant profit increases.

Another report, *Women in Business and Management: The business case for change*, surveyed almost 13,000 enterprises in 70 countries. More than 57 per cent of respondents agreed that gender diversity initiatives improved business outcomes. Almost three-quarters of those companies that tracked gender diversity in their management, reported profit increases of between 5 and 20 per cent, with the majority seeing increases of between 10 and 15 percent.

"We expected to see a positive correlation between gender diversity and business success," said Deborah France-Massin, Director of the ILO Bureau for Employers' Activities, "but these results are eye-opening… the significance is clear. Companies should look at gender balance as a bottom-line issue, not just a human resource issue. The business case for getting more women into management is compelling."

MANY WOMEN IN LEADERSHIP
=
FINER ART

Women have been trained to speak softly
and carry a lipstick.
Those days are over.
\-   Bella Abzug

Art is of critical significance to the well-being of
communities and societies. Art tells a people's stories,
expresses thought and feeling, describes notions of
beauty and harmony, reinforces and renews culture, and
communicates political, spiritual or philosophical

ideas, among other things. Art is real, art is subjective and some art is functional.

Olufar Elliason believes that engaging with a good work of art can connect people to their senses, body, and mind. Art does not show people what to do, but it can make the world *felt*, and that this "felt" feeling might spur thinking, engagement, and even action. He believes that most people know the feeling of being moved by a work of art, whether it is a song, a play, a poem, a novel, a painting, or a spatio-temporal experiment and he also believes that one of the major responsibilities of artists…is to help people not only get to know and understand something with their minds, but also to feel it emotionally and physically.

Art, at its root, is an expression and the artist is an expresser, translating feeling in order to create meaning. Art expresses and translates, art acknowledges and reveals, art transfers and art intervenes. Art is an expression of feeling, belief, and character.

Yet, "Women in the Visual Arts" from Oxford Art Online, says that, "From ancient times to the present, women throughout the world have participated in the visual arts in diverse and stimulating ways. Whether as creators and innovators of numerous forms of artistic expression, important patrons and collectors, or significant contributors to the discipline of art history, women have been and continue to be integral to the institution of art. For the most part, however, traditional art history has systematically excluded or masked women's participation in the visual arts. Instead of recognizing the social barriers to entry that women have faced when trying to engage with the art world, the discipline has historically deemed women's contributions as non-existent or inferior to those of men."

Writing for "SmartHistory" Dr. Deana McDonald observes that, "When Renaissance painter Plautilla Nelli got her first solo exhibit at Florence's Uffizi Gallery in 2017, some art historians asked . . . Plautilla who?? Despite being a celebrated artist in sixteenth-century Florence, Nelli had been forgotten by art history to the point that even scholars of Renaissance art knew nothing of her. How was this possible? In a word, gender. Nelli's obscurity was the cumulative effect of historical gender imbalances that limited women in the Renaissance and modern art worlds."

In 1550, and again in 1568, Florentine painter, engineer, architect, writer and historian, Giorgio Vasari, published a series of biographies of artists of his time, which some researchers consider "the first important book on art history" ever written. Originally titled, *Le Vite de'Piv Eccellenti Pittori Scultori et Architettori* – in English, *Lives of the Most Excellent Painters, Sculptors and Architects* – it is now commonly referred to simply as, "The Lives". The biography of Madonna Properzia de' Rossi, a sculptor, which he included, says everything that need be said, in this book, even today, almost five centuries later, about women's leadership in the arts or in any other area, so I simply include it here for your edification, with both gratitude and credit to the writer himself, and translators various.

Properzia de' Rossi is the only woman to whom Vasari dedicated one of his biographies, but in it, he mentions many other women of accomplishment, and begins, as the reader will see, with the observation that, "It is an extraordinary thing that in all those arts and all those exercises wherein at any time women have thought fit to play a part in real earnest, they have always become most excellent and famous in no common way, as one might easily demonstrate by an endless number of examples."

He laments that Sister Plautilla, a nun and Prioress in the Convent of Santa Caterina da
Siena – and other women, presumably – would have done marvelous things "if she had enjoyed, as men do, advantages for studying, devoting herself to drawing, and copying living and natural objects."

Lives of the Most Excellent Painters, Sculptors and Architects by Giorgio Vasari

It is an extraordinary thing that in all those arts and all those exercises wherein at any time women have thought fit to play a part in real earnest, they have always become most excellent and famous in no common way, as one might easily demonstrate by an endless number of examples. Everyone, indeed, knows what they are all, without exception, worth in household matters; besides which, in connection with war, likewise, it is known who were Camilla, Harpalice, Valasca, Tomyris, Penthesilea, Molpadia, Orizia, Antiope, Hippolyta, Semiramis, Zenobia, and, finally, Mark Antony's Fulvia, who so often took up arms, as the historian Dion tells us, to defend her husband and herself. But in poetry, also, they have been truly marvelous, as Pausanias relates. Corinna was very celebrated as a writer of verse, and Eustathius makes mention in his "Catalogue of the Ships of Homer" – as does Eusebius in his book of "Chronicles" – of Sappho, a young woman of great renown, who, in truth, although she was a woman, was yet such that she surpassed by a great measure all the eminent writers of that age.

And Varro, on his part, gives extraordinary but well-deserved praise to Erinna, who, with her three hundred verses, challenged the fame of the brightest light of Greece, and counterbalanced with her one small volume, called the "Elecate," the ponderous "Iliad" of the great Homer. Aristophanes celebrates Carissena, a votary of the same profession, as a woman of great excellence and learning; and the same may be said for Teano, Merone, Polla, Elpe, Cornificia, and Telesilla, to the last of whom, in honor of her marvelous talents, a most beautiful statue was set up in the Temple of Venus.

Passing by the numberless other writers of verse, do we not read that Arete was the teacher of the learned Aristippus in the difficulties of philosophy, and that Lastheneia and Assiotea were disciples of the divine Plato? In the art of oratory, Sempronia and Hortensia, women of Rome, were very famous. In grammar, so Athenaeus relates, Agallis was without an equal. And as for the prediction of the future, whether we class this with astrology or with magic, it is enough to say that Themis, Cassandra, and Manto had an extraordinary renown in their times; as did Isis and Ceres in matters of agriculture, and the Thespiades in the whole field of the sciences.

But in no other age, for certain, has it been possible to see this better than in our own, wherein women have won the highest fame not only in the study of letters-- as has been done by Signora Vittoria del Vasto, Signora Veronica Gambara, Signora Caterina Anguisciuola, Schioppa, Nugarola, Madonna Laura Battiferri, and a hundred others, all most learned as well in the vulgar tongue as in the Latin and the Greek-- but also in every other faculty. Nor have they been too proud to set themselves with their little hands, so tender and so white, as if to wrest from us the palm of supremacy, to manual labors, braving the roughness of marble and the unkindly chisels, in order to attain to their desire and thereby win fame; as did, in our own day, Properzia de' Rossi of Bologna, a young woman excellent not only in household matters, like the rest of them, but also in sciences without number, so that all the men, to say nothing of the women, were envious of her.

This Properzia was very beautiful in person, and played and sang in her day better than any other woman of her city. And because she had an intellect both capricious and very ready, she set herself to carve peach-stones, which she executed so well and with such patience, that they were singular and marvelous to behold, not only for the subtlety of the work, but also for the grace of the little figures that she made in them and the delicacy with which they were distributed. And it was certainly a miracle to see on so small a thing as a peach-stone the whole Passion of Christ, wrought in most beautiful carving, with a vast number of figures in addition to the Apostles and the ministers of the Crucifixion.

This encouraged her, since there were decorations to be made for the three doors of the first facade of S. Petronio all in figures of marble, to ask the Wardens of Works, by means of her husband, for a part of that work; at which they were quite content, on the condition that she should let them see some work in marble executed by her own hand. Whereupon upon she straightway made for Count Alessandro de' Peppoli a portrait from life in the finest marble, representing his father, Count Guido, which gave infinite pleasure not only to them, but also to the whole city; and the Wardens of Works, therefore, did not fail to allot a part of the work to her.

In this, to the vast delight of all Bologna, she made an exquisite scene, wherein--because at that time the poor woman was madly enamoured of a handsome young man, who seemed to care but little for her--she represented the wife of Pharaoh's Chamberlain, who, burning with love for Joseph, and almost in despair after so much persuasion, finally strips his garment from him with a womanly grace that defies description. This work was esteemed by all to be most beautiful, and it was a great satisfaction to herself, thinking that with this illustration from the Old Testament she had partly quenched the raging fire of her own passion. Nor would she ever do any more work in connection with that building, although there was no person who did not beseech her that she should go on with it, save only Maestro Amico, who out of envy always dissuaded her and went so far with his malignity, ever speaking ill of her to the Wardens, that she was paid a most beggarly price for her work.

She also made two angels in very strong relief and beautiful proportions, which may now be seen, although against her wish , in the same building. In the end she devoted herself to copper-plate engraving, which she did without reproach, gaining the highest praise. And so the poor love-stricken young woman came to succeed most perfectly in everything, save in her unhappy passion.

The fame of an intellect so noble and so exalted spread throughout all Italy, and finally came to the ears of Pope Clement VII, who, immediately after he had crowned the Emperor in Bologna, made inquiries after her; but he found that the poor woman had died that very week, and had been buried in the Della Morte Hospital, as she had directed in her last testament. At which the Pope, who was eager to see her, felt much sorrow at her death; but more bitter even was it for her fellow-citizens, who regarded her during her lifetime as one of the greatest miracles produced by nature in our days.

In our book are some very good drawings by the hand of this Properzia, done with the pen and copied from the works of Raffaello da Urbino; and her portrait was given to me by certain painters who were very much her friends. But, although Properzia drew very well, there have not been wanting women not only to equal her in drawing, but also to do as good work in painting as she did in sculpture. Of these the first is Sister Plautilla, a nun and now Prioress in the Convent of Santa Caterina da Siena, on the Piazza di San Marco in Florence. She, beginning little by little to draw and to imitate in colors pictures and paintings by excellent masters, has executed some works with such diligence, that she has caused the craftsmen to marvel.

By her hand are two panels in the Church of that Convent of Santa Caterina, of which the one with the Magi adoring Jesus is much extolled. In the choir of the Convent of Santa Lucia, at Pistoia, there is a large panel, containing Our Lady with the Child in her arms, St. Thomas, St. Augustine, St. Mary Magdalene, St. Catherine of Siena, St. Agnes, St. Catherine the Martyr, and St. Lucia; and another large panel by the same hand was sent abroad by the Director of the Hospital of Lelmo. In the refectory of the aforesaid Convent of Santa Caterina there is a great Last Supper, with a panel in the workroom, both by the hand of the same nun.

And in the houses of gentlemen throughout Florence there are so many pictures, that it would be tedious to attempt to speak of them all. A large picture of the Annunciation belongs to the wife of the Spaniard, Signor Mondragone, and Madonna Marietta de' Fedini has another like it. There is a little picture of Our Lady in San Giovannino, at Florence; and an altar-predella in Santa Maria del Fiore, containing very beautiful scenes from the life of San Zanobi. And because this venerable and talented sister, before executing panels and works of importance, gave attention to painting in miniature, there are in the possession of various people many wonderfully beautiful little pictures by her hand, of which there is no need to make mention.

The best works from her hand are those that she has copied from others, wherein she shows that she would have done marvelous things if she had enjoyed, as men do, advantages for studying, devoting herself to drawing, and copying living and natural objects. And that this is true is seen clearly from a picture of the Nativity of Christ, copied from one which Bronzino once painted for Filippo Salviati. In like manner the truth of such an opinion is proved by this, that in her works the faces and features of women, whom she has been able to see as much as she pleased, are no little better than the heads of the men, and much nearer to the reality. In the faces of women in some of her works she has portrayed Madonna Costanza de' Doni, who has been in our time an unexampled pattern of beauty and dignity; painting her so well, that it is impossible to expect more from a woman who, for the reasons mentioned above, has had no great practice in her art.

With much credit to herself, likewise, has Madonna Lucrezia, the daughter of Messer Alfonso Quistelli della Mirandola, and now the wife of Count Clemente Pietra, occupied herself with drawing and painting, as she still does, after having been taught by Alessandro Allori, the pupil of Bronzino; as may be seen from many pictures and portraits executed by her hand, which are worthy to be praised by all. But Sofonisba of Cremona , the daughter of Messer Amilcaro Anguisciuola, has labored at the difficulties of design with greater study and better grace than any other woman of our time, and she has not only succeeded in drawing, coloring, and copying from nature, and in making excellent copies of works by other hands, but has also executed by herself alone some very choice and beautiful works of painting.

Wherefore she well deserved that King Philip of Spain, having heard of her merits and abilities from the Lord Duke of Alba, should have sent for her and caused her to be escorted in great honor to Spain, where he keeps her with a rich allowance about the person of the Queen, to the admiration of all that Court, which reveres the excellence of Sofonisba as a miracle. And it is no long time since Messer Tommaso Cavalieri, a Roman gentle man, sent to the Lord Duke Cosimo (in addition to a drawing by the hand of the divine Michelangelo, wherein is a Cleopatra) another drawing by the hand of Sofonisba, containing a little girl laughing at a boy who is weeping because one of the crayfish out of a basket full of them, which she has placed in front of him, is biting his finger; and there is nothing more graceful to be seen than that drawing, or more true to nature.

Wherefore, in memory of the talent of Sofonisba, who lives in Spain, so that Italy has no abundance of

her works, I have placed it in my book of drawings. We may truly say, then, with the divine Ariosto, that
Le donne son venute in eccellenza
   Di ciascun' arte ov' hanno posto cura.

The book of Esther in the Christian Holy Book, the Bible, tells the story that on the seventh day of a feast being given by King Ahasuerus of Persia, the king, having had too much wine, gave an order to seven of his eunuchs to bring Queen Vashti before him, wearing only her royal crown. He wanted to show off her naked beauty to his vassals in attendance. Queen Vashti refused. She was banished, therefore, and eventually replaced by Esther.

Ahasuerus kept eunuchs in his employ, as did many royal and imperial courts of those times, because they were considered safer for some duties than were other men. Believed to be free from the influence of testosterone, they were trusted to not dally with the king's women, and they were therefore often also assigned to guard the harem. Eunuchs were unable to father offspring and therefore were also considered less likely to present a dynastic challenge for the ruler.

A eunuch is a man who has been castrated, to serve a specific social function. Some of the earliest records of men being intentionally castrated date back to the twenty-first century BCE in Sumeria. These were generally boys and men of the lower social classes who were then considered safe to be entrusted with these courtiers' duties, and royal servants' assignments. They were bedchamber attendants, government officials, royal guards and trusted soldiers. Some were religious specialists and singers.

Many centuries ago, there developed in Western Europe, a specialized group of singing eunuchs who were known as "i castrati". Women in Western Europe, were also sequestered in many respects, restricted in their independent movements and generally not allowed participation in public activities. They were especially not permitted activity in the theatre or in the church. The Pauline dictum, *mulieres in ecclesiis taceant* or "let women keep silent in the churches", banned women even from singing in the church choir! But the best music called for a range of voices, which had to include the higher-pitched female tones.

Young boys were, therefore, trained to sing and then were castrated while still very young, before their voices "broke", so as to preserve the feminine, high-pitched tones. Choirs of these "castrati" sang in the Hagia Sophia and in the Sistine Chapel. In 1589, by the papal bull *Cum pro nostro pastorali munere*, Pope Sixtus V re-organised the choir of St. Peter's in Rome, specifically to include castrati. Some records claim that during the 1720s and 1730s, at the height of the craze for these voices, upwards of 4,000 boys were castrated each year, in the service of art.

Over time, the times changed and eventually, the barbaric practice was discontinued. Castration was officially made illegal after the unification of Italy in 1861. The practice was maintained in the Catholic Church until 1903, however. Even so, when the new pope, Pius X, who was the Head of the Catholic Church from 1903 to 1914, issued his *motu proprio, Tra le Sollecitudini* ('Amongst the Cares'), it still contained the instruction: It follows that, singers in church have a real liturgical office, and that therefore, women being incapable of exercising such office, cannot be admitted to form part of the choir. Whenever, then, it is desirable to employ the high voices of sopranos and contraltos, these parts must be taken by boys, according to the most ancient usage of the Church.

Eventually, however, women were allowed to sing in public and in church, and many women do nowadays make a living from this activity – and a very good one too, in many cases. In the seventeenth century, with the advent of Opera, women had begun to be included in theatre and did sometimes sing, but until quite recently, the Catholic Church continued to consider it impure and improper for women to be on the stage.

Today, women are amongst the leaders in the music industry, both secular and religious. They are rock stars, bandleaders, choir mistresses, solo artists, opera singers, conductors of orchestras, producers of concerts. With no need anymore, to rely on anyone's permission, they engage in a whole host of other music-related pursuits – and provide work and money for many, many men.

Fast forward to: Amelita Galli-Curuci, Giulietta Simionato, Lotte Lehmann, Montserrat

Caballe, Maria Callas, Leontyne Price, Fiorenza Cossotto, Joan Sutherland, Kiri Te Kawana,

Jessye Norman, Cecilia Bartoli, Angela Gheorghiu…and this is merely the beginnings of a very long list.

We could also add singers of more "popular" music: Edith Piaf, Aretha Franklyn, Milva,

Barbra Streisand, Mina, Shirley Bassey, Ella Fitzgerald, Emel Mathlouthi, Amy Winehouse,

Fan Bingbing, Dolly Parton, Miriam Makeba, Cesaria Evora, Katsutaro Kauta, Angelique Kidjo, Kimiko Kasai, Yasmin Hamdan, Faye Wong, Umm Kulthum, Nina Simone, Asia Madani…the list is endless.

Young boys no longer are castrated in the service of art, sacrificed to uphold the patriarchy's fear of women, and the world of music is all the better for this.

It is well-known that in Shakespeare's Globe Theatre, even the most complex female roles he wrote were mostly played by teenaged boys. Of course, Shakespeare's plays were rife with dirty jokes and double entendre, social intercourse still considered, by some, to be not fit fare for ladies! Furthermore, women were prohibited, by law, from appearing on stage, anyway. Although Western theatre traditions had their genesis in Greece as far back as 532 BCE, the Greeks themselves had also considered it "dangerous" for women to perform in public, so they had not been allowed on stage there either. It was men who played the parts of women in these early works. Things were only very slightly better with the Romans.

France did not legally restrict women from performing on stage, but the Catholic Church thought it morally wrong, and actors – male and female – were routinely excommunicated.

Up until the 1630s, "an honest woman" did not even go to the theatre. Seventeenth century

French society did not resist that. When a furious Cardinal Richelieu accused the poet Boisrobert of allowing "a whore" to contaminate his theatre, Boisrobert having invited an actress to watch a rehearsal in the Palais-Cardinal, the poet is reputed to have responded, "I only know her as an actress, I've never seen her except on the stage, where Your Eminence put her…" but he then added, "I believe they are all whores, and I don't believe there have ever been any who were not."

Professor Virginia Scott at the University of Massachusetts, Amherst, has written that, "As far back as Xenophon in the fourth century bce, women who performed for money, publicly or privately, faced the condescension and contempt of their societies."

"During the Victorian period, men's and women's roles became more sharply defined than at any time in (British) history," writes Kathryn Hughes, Professor of Lifewriting and Convenor of the MA in Lifewriting at the University of East Anglia in the UK. And these attitudes were not restricted to Britain; they were enforced and made to take hold across much of the British colonized world, and beyond.

Paradoxically, performance skills, an ease with and knowledge of art, were considered valuable proficiencies for women, but for the very specific purpose of enticing a man and bringing about a marriage. "Rather than attracting a husband through their domestic abilities," writes Hughes, "middle-class girls were coached in what were known as "accomplishments".

In Jane Austen's Pride & Prejudice, Caroline Bingley lists the skills required by any young lady who considered herself accomplished. "A woman must have a thorough knowledge of music, singing, drawing, dancing, and the modern languages," she said. But, of course, a lady was never allowed to play an instrument, sing or – God forbid! – dance for the public. Even with personal guests in the drawing rooms of private homes, there were well-established and socially-enforced limits to what a 'lady' could do. For a time, dancing, for example, followed very formal rules whereby women entered upon the dance floor only on the arm of a partner who had previously "booked" his dance. He did this by adding his name, having formally received permission to do so, to the list on the dance cards, or *programme du bal,* kept by women for that express purpose – and monitored by chaperones, mothers and governesses.

Japanese kabuki is a theatre art form said to have been developed by a female temple dancer name Okuni, yet today, kabuki is male performance art. Female performers were banned from kabuki in 1629 and that ban lasted until the Meiji Restoration in 1868. However, women are still very much excluded even today. Japanese society has long been very precisely delineated. The rulers of Japanese society have demanded absolute adherence to the hierarchical structures prescribed by Confucianism, and following these same rules, members of the society were expected to not deviate from the rules and not push the boundaries.

Kabuki was a commoner's art form, created for ordinary townspeople, but from its very inception, it had always attracted an audience from every stratum of society. The themes of the dramas and dances were taken from everyday life, but the performances – and equally, the performers – were very attractive all across the spectrum and the public response to that attraction, occasioned considerable disturbance in Japanese society.

The dances were choreographed not only to show off the dancer's skills but to titillate and charm the audience, with the aim of the performer's acquiring a customer afterwards. Prostitution was common in Japan in the early days of the development of the art form and temple dancers like Okuni were often also prostitutes. So it is that, from the outset, kabuki was associated with prostitution and from its beginnings, has relied heavily on eroticism, beauty and androgyny to captivate its audience. Samurai and merchants alike competed for the favours of kabuki dancers, spending a lot of money for these favours, engaging in violence over their preferred dancers, and in these relationships, blurring the lines between the classes.

This mixing – and rivalry – brought about between members of the different classes, by these unique characteristics of kabuki – was unwelcome to the country's rulers. This blending and blurring of lines was not at all pleasing to the shogun. So, in 1629, partly to restore social order and to try to stem the violence between merchants and samurai, the government issued its first ban on women acting in kabuki. That change brought no less violence and no improvement in the social behaviours, because men fought over the young boys to quite the same degree. The government therefore banned the boys who had taken the place of the women. Kabuki did not die, however, and it took a while, but eventually kabuki came to have only adult male actors, and with only a few exceptions, that is still very much the case to this day.

The first American playhouse, or theatre, was opened in 1716 in Williamsburg, Virginia, by William Levingston, a merchant. It was not immediately popular. There was growing abhorrence in regard to British rule and culture at the time, and theatre was viewed as an example of British indecency and immorality. There was great concern, among the men who made up the ruling and clerical classes, over the moral implications of both acting in and viewing plays, so theatre was very strenuously resisted. Massachusetts and Pennsylvania even passed laws to forbid the production and performance of plays.

The Articles of Association passed by the first Continental Congress, called for a *"discountenance and discourage [of] every species of extravagance and dissipation, especially... exhibitions of shows, plays, and other expensive diversions."* George Fox, founder and leader of the Quaker faith, wrote that he believed that music and the stage *"burthened the pure life, and stirred up the people's vanity,"* implying that he believed theatre made it impossible for people to lead a "pure" life in pursuit of God. The history of American theatre, as recorded by Arcadia Publishing, tells that as theatre slowly took root, *"Types of productions during this time period varied widely..."* and *"minstrel shows dominated as the popular entertainment form."*

Of course, women were prohibited for the same reasons as they were in other parts of the world, but as the years passed, the restrictions were slowly ground down, and there came many women in the theatre audiences, and female playwrights, actors and musical arrangers and directors. An excerpt from *Women In Theatre* published by the University of Virginia reads, "In his book Actresses and Suffragists, Albert Auster contends that "the 1890s were a period of pre-eminence for theatre in American society and culture." By 1900 there were 3000 theatres in the United States and with industry producing at peak levels, the increase in leisure time and disposable income translated into a swell in the popularity of the stage.

What is often overlooked, not surprisingly, is the role that women played in the rise of theatre. Women were not only attending plays in record numbers but were finding positions in chorus lines and as featured actresses.

Today, there are women all around the world who are leading actors in every aspect of theatre. There are women performers and producers, directors and doorkeepers; women financers, teachers, scouts and writers, and more. Women in leadership in theatre has made theatre better universally, without question.

With the development of photography, theatre progressed into film, or "motion pictures" as it was originally called. An article written in National Geographic by Pedro Garcia Martin, says, "Auguste and Louis Lumière invented a camera that could record, develop, and project film, but they regarded their creation as little more than a curious novelty. Shortly after the public premiere of their first film, Louis was said to have remarked: "Le cinéma est une invention sans avenir." Translation: Cinema is an invention without a future."

In an article titled, *9 Women Who Were Motion Picture Pioneers*, Brett Leveridge writes that for much of its history, Hollywood has been something of a boy's club. He also affirms that this had not always been the case, but that in the early years, women were major contributors to the motion picture industry – and not only onscreen. It was a woman, Dorothy Arzner, who cobbled together the first boom mic by hanging a microphone from a fishing pole. She was also the first film editor to receive a screen credit.

Mary Pickford has been called, "The Woman Who Shaped Hollywood". "Before Pickford," says the BBC, "the movies were disreputable." With Douglas Fairbanks, Charlie Chaplin and D.W. Griffith, Pickford created United Artists in 1919, a move which took the power back from business men and returned into the hands of the artists. United Artists was the first major production company to be controlled by its artists rather than by businessmen. Pickford was also one of the original founders of the Academy of Motion Picture Arts and Sciences which confers the annual Oscars.

Margaret Talbot writes in The New Yorker that, "One of the stranger things about the history of moviemaking is that women have been there all along, periodically exercising real power behind the camera, yet their names and contributions keep disappearing, as though security had been called, again and again, to escort them from the set. In the early years of the twentieth century, women worked in virtually every aspect of silent-film-making, as directors, writers, producers, editors, and even camera operators. The industry – new, ad hoc, making up its own rules as it went along – had not yet locked in a strict division of labor by gender. Women came to Los Angeles from all over the country, impelled not so much by dreams of stardom as by the prospect of interesting work in a freewheeling enterprise that valued them."

"Of all the different industries that have offered opportunities to women," the screenwriter Clara Beranger told an interviewer in 1919, "none have given them the chance that motion pictures have."

Alice Blaché, born in France in 1873, directed some six hundred movie shorts in her lifetime. In 1914, she wrote, "There is nothing connected with the staging of a motion picture that a woman cannot do as easily as a man, and there is no reason why she cannot completely master every technicality of the art."

Talbot comments, "As the film industry became an increasingly modern, capitalist enterprise, consolidated around a small number of leading studios, each with specialized departments, it grew harder for women…" Many other commentators contend that the quality of film had degenerated in those years, also, the focus being more on quantity of business and less on quality of art.

Antonia Lant, who has co-edited a book of women's writing in early cinema, observes, "By the 1930s, we find a powerful case of forgetting, forgetting that so many women had even held the posts of director and producer." Zora Neale Hurston, for example, could actually be, according to Gloria Gibson, the first African-American woman filmmaker. But she had been completely forgotten until in 1975, *Ms.* Magazine published Alice Walker's article *"In Search of Zora Neale Hurston."*

A study by the Center for the Study of Women in Television and Film at San Diego University has found that the number of women working in the US film industry reached an historic high in 2019, but that men still outnumber women four to one in key roles. Women make up twenty percent of behind-the-scenes roles…and when it comes to key jobs like director and cinematographer, men continue to dominate.

In 2019, the report says, females accounted for thirty-seven percent of major characters, up just one percentage point from thirty-six percent in 2018, and thirty-four percent of all speaking characters, down one percentage point from thirty-five in 2018.

Regarding race and ethnicity, the percentage of Black females in speaking roles declined slightly from twenty-one percent in 2018 to twenty in 2019.

By role, on the top two hundred and fifty films, women comprised nineteen percent of writers, twenty-one percent of executive producers, twenty-seven of producers, twenty-three percent of editors and five of cinematographers; six percent of composers, forty of music supervisors; nine percent of supervising sound editors and four of sound designers; twenty-three percent of production designers, thirty-one of art directors, four of special effects supervisors, and six percent of visual effects supervisors.

In 2018, women comprised just four percent of directors working on the top one hundred films, eight percent on the top two hundred and fifty, and fifteen percent on the top five hundred. The Hollywood Reporter reports that one key to boosting the number of women on a production was having a female director. Among the top 500 films, it says, those with at least one female director, women made up 71 percent of writers, 47 percent of editors, 19 percent of cinematographers and 24 percent of composers.

Greg Kilday writes in The Hollywood Reporter article, "The year 2018 appeared to mark the beginning of dramatic changes for women working behind the camera on Hollywood movies" With Disney's *A Wrinkle in Time,* Ava DuVernay had become the first black woman to direct a big budget one hundred million dollar movie, Patty Jenkins had had great success with 2017's *Wonder Woman,* Anna Boden had co-directed Marvel's upcoming *Captain Marvel,* and Cathy Yan was the lead on *Birds of Prey* for DC and Warners.

Despite such high-profile breakthroughs, continues Kilday, the statistics tell a different story. A survey of the top 250 films of 2018 at the domestic box office found that women made up just 8 percent of the directors involved, a number that was down 3 percentage points
from the 11 percent in 2017. It's also 1 percent below the 9 percent recorded 10 years ago, in 1998. The percentages of women directing films in the top 100 and top 500 films declined as well.

The data across all the awards also tells an all-too familiar story of gender exclusion whether it's Cannes' Palme d'Or, Switzerland's Locarno Film Festival, Hollywood's Oscars, the UK's BAFTA, Nigeria's Nollywood, or India's Bollywood.

"Sometimes women can't ask for control, so they have to take it. Ok? I want you to remember that," says Alex Levy, a character on Apple TV's star-studded new drama The Morning Show.

In the many places where movies are made these days, women are taking their place – claiming their place – and doing spectacular work. There are, e.g. Ava DuVernay, Sofia Coppola, Salma Hayek, Kathryn Bigelow, Oprah Winfrey, Eva Longoria, Nicole Kidman, Kemi Adetiba, Rene Liu Ruo-ying, Su Lun, Shelly Chopra Dhar…and many others leading the charge every day behind the scenes and in front of the cameras to change the statistics and the reality of the film industry worldwide – to everybody's greater benefit.

MANY WOMEN IN LEADERSHIP

=

BETTER GOVERNMENT

Some leaders are born women.

\-   Geraldine Ferraro

Only five percent of the countries in the world are currently led by a woman. Eleven women are serving as Head of State and twelve are serving as Head of Government.

Of national parliamentarians, only twenty-four point three percent are women. There are only three countries in the whole world, where women make up fifty percent or more of the members of parliament.

There are twenty-seven states in which women account for less than ten percent of parliamentarians in single or lower houses, including three chambers where there is not even one woman in any office.

This scenario persists despite established and growing evidence that women's leadership in political decision-making processes improves these processes and their outcomes. Experts say that when women are better represented in government office, the gains are likely to spill down and elevate the lives of all women and improve communities, and consequently make things better for the society in general.

Women's representation makes a difference in local and national governments. One of the most effective ways in which women demonstrate political leadership is by working across party lines through parliamentary women's caucuses, even in the most politically combative environments. Women work together to champion issues of gender equality, such as the elimination of gender-based violence, parental leave and childcare, pensions, gender-equality laws and electoral reform. One notable exception to this rule is provided by Britain's Margaret Thatcher, the first woman to become leader of the Conservative Party and Prime Minister. Julie Bindel writes, "She was a female politician promulgating male politics."

"There is strong evidence that as more women are elected to office, there are more policies enacted that emphasise quality of life and reflect the priorities of families, women and minorities," Katja Iversen, president of WomenDeliver, told IPS News.

WomenDeliver is an international organisation advocating around the world for gender equality and the health and rights of girls and women. Part of its work is to harness evidence and unite diverse voices to spark commitment to gender equality. "Studies also show," said Iversen, "that women are more likely than men to work across party lines, help secure lasting peace, and prioritise health, education and other societal priorities which are key to the wellbeing and prosperity of both (the women's) constituents and societies at large."

UN Women research on *panchayats* (local councils) in India, discovered that the number of drinking water projects in areas with women-led councils was 62 per cent higher than in those with men-led councils. In Norway, a direct causal relationship was found between the presence of women in municipal councils and childcare coverage for families.

Currently, Latin America is leading globally in local and parliamentary positions held by women. Women hold twenty-seven percent of local positions as council members or councillors, in the group of countries in the region, an increase of 6.5 per cent in the last 10 years, but the journey to political participation has not been easy for female politicians in Latin America. It is fraught with rising violence and intimidation against women in politics, UN Women reports. Harassment, threats and even death, have made it a risky career choice. This is true even in ground-breaking Bolivia, which has continued to hold on to its position at the top of the list for many years now. In 2014, Bolivia held the number three spot; women accounted for 53.1 per cent of Parliamentarians and 44.1 per cent of local councillors. These positives have remained for this country.

Dr. Thoraya Obaid, former Executive Director of the United Nations Population Fund, was the first Arab woman to head a UN agency. Writing for Women Political Leaders, she says, "We know that all policy decisions have gender ramifications and that is why gender mainstreaming must occur at the beginning of the policy making process or we risk maintaining the status quo of exclusive decision-making which is only representative of half of the society."

Founded by Silvana Koch-Mehrin of Iceland, Women Political Leaders describes itself as "the global network of female politicians." The organisation says it believes that progress happens by convening women political leaders who have the drive and the influence to create positive change, and that it strives in all its activities to demonstrate the impact of more women in political leadership, for the global better.

In April 2018, Abiy Ahmed was elected Prime Minister of Ethiopia. He revolutionised government in his country by appointing women to fill full half of his government's ministerial posts, including the job of defence minister, which is universally, traditionally one for the men. Explaining his decision in a speech to Parliament, Mr Abiy said women had made a great contribution to restoring peace and stability in the country, were less corrupt than men, respected their work and could sustain the drive for change.

Aisha Mohammed became Ethiopia's first female defence minister and Muferiat Kamil, the former Speaker of Parliament, was made the country's first Minister of Peace. She oversees the country's intelligence and security apparatus, including the federal police. SahleWork Zewde became the first woman president of Ethiopia.

Hadra Ahmed, an Ethiopian journalist, tells IPS News that Ethiopians strongly believe women can never be as good as men. She said that the messages come from the whole system. The system demonstrates and reinforces this perspective through the application of different policies such as affirmative action that lowers the passing grade for girls, rather than helping them to study and making sure they make it to school on time. Even mothers and influential people tell women and girls that they are not as capable as men and boys

"Women are powerful agents of change, and their participation at all decision-making levels is a prerequisite for politics and programs that reflect societies and are effective, sustainable and inclusive," said Iversen.

The new gender-equal government in Ethiopia, is already making changes that directly impact women's lives and livelihoods. The country now has a new law that has annulled previous legal provisions that gave a husband full control over a couple's assets and full authority to decide whether his wife could work outside of the home. As a result, spouses are now equal with regard to the administration of assets, and a husband cannot unilaterally, legally, prevent his wife from working.

The challenges for Ethiopian women endure, but change is clearly afoot even beyond the political level. Setaweet, the country's first feminist research and training company, has set up offices in Addis Ababa, the Ethiopian capital. The company offers tailor-made gender equality services for schools, agencies and corporations. Its flagship project is a feminist curriculum for secondary school students dealing with femininity and masculinity, healthy relationships and positive self-images.

In 2005, Angela Merkel became the first female chancellor of the Federal Republic of Germany. She has since been dubbed Queen of Germany, and even Empress of Europe. The BBC says that she cultivated the image of a prudent and pragmatic leader, and Deutsche Welle (DW), the major German public media company, remarks that she fundamentally changed the country and was often praised for her calm demeanour, though her time in power has, nonetheless, been turbulent.

Chancellor Merkel has less power as political leader than the French, Russian or US heads of government, DW reports, but she has profoundly impacted Germany during her years in charge. Under Merkel's reign, Germany's economy prospered, despite the global financial crisis of 2007-08. Germany, which as recently as 2005 was still known as the "sick man of Europe," re-emerged as an economic growth engine. Over time, German unemployment fell by half, and tax revenue grew. Germany's move in 2009 to adopt a balanced-budget provision, marked a paradigm shift that literally paid off: in the years since, the country has gone from public deficit to comfortable surplus.

German media generally, has also declared itself impressed with her abilities. Her leadership has brought about the transformation of the German capital into a hot spot of European diplomacy through her engagement with regard to the eurozone crisis, the Greek bailout and Russia's annexation of Ukraine's Crimean Peninsula. The chancellor has proven herself a skilled conflict manager, and is held in high esteem by the German people, not least because over the course of her terms in office, young, female party members were encouraged to rise up the ranks, and they have changed the party – and, through this, the country.

When other government leaders were waffling and indecisive about the stream of refugees seeking asylum from wars and unrest in Africa and the Middle East, her response was, "We can do it!" indicating with those few words, that Germany was open to taking in hundreds of thousands of asylum-seekers from Syria and neighbouring war-torn regions.

Chancellor Merkel has been one of the women leaders of countries to have received praise and acknowledgement for her handling of the coronavirus pandemic. The latest Deutschlandtrend survey by Infratest dimap, shows that two-thirds of respondents give the government positive marks for its handling of the coronavirus crisis.

In the United States, Senator Kamala Harris was selected to become the vice-president should former vice-president Joe Biden win his campaign for the presidency. She had previously launched her own bid for the Democratic Party's nomination for president, but in the words of Voice of America (VOA) she was unable to "maintain her standing in the retail give-and-take politicking of an American presidential campaign." Also according to the VOA, "of the three women previously on U.S. national political tickets — two vice presidential candidates, and 2016 Democratic presidential candidate Hillary Clinton — all lost. If the Biden-Harris ticket wins, Harris would become the highest-ranking female U.S. official in the country's 244-year history."

As Senator, Harris was a member of the Senate Judiciary Committee. She had sparred with Trump administration officials and pointedly questioned Neil Gorsuch and Brett Kavanaugh, the two conservative nominees to the Supreme Court under Trump, and sharply questioned Attorney General William Barr. She voted against both Supreme Court nominees. The year Harris entered the US Senate, a Quorum case study noted this: In the 114th Congress, female lawmakers hold a record 104 seats—the first time in history that the number of women in Congress has surpassed 100, out of a total of 535 seats – 435 in the House of Representatives and 100 in the Senate.

Looking back over the last seven years, insights from Quorum show that this unprecedented female representation may have led to more legislative activity as female Members of Congress not only work more frequently with each other, but also work more frequently across the aisle, passing more legislation in the Senate than their male colleagues. Furthermore, in recent years, female senators have demonstrated more bipartisanship with their female colleagues than their male counterparts.

Harris herself has worked on politically bipartisan pieces of legislation with Republicans. Republican Sen. Lindsey Graham of South Carolina, a Washington veteran of more almost twenty years and a Trump supporter, has said of Harris, "She's hard-nosed. She's smart. She's tough."

Joe Biden did, indeed, win the election to the presidency and Harris sworn in as the first woman Vice-president of the United States. Her campaign as part of the Biden/Harris ticket was fuelled in large part by women determined to usher in a new era in America politics and relations. Her accession is being celebrated in many countries around the world in the expectation that it will be an opening for women, that she herself will be able to inspire and help drive support for the advancement of women to positions of leadership in all sectors of society.

In 2016, The Atlantic published an article the title of which asked the question, *Would Electing More Women Fix Congress?* The first paragraph of the article reads, "Only nineteen percent of the seats in the U.S.

Congress are held by women, despite the fact that women make up more than half the United States' population. Congress being what it is these days— a snarling ragebeast incapable of compromise—it's an easy jump to wonder if this wild gender imbalance might be part of the problem." Yet, the answer offered in the piece is, "If every man in the Capitol were replaced with a woman, we couldn't say for certain that more bills would be passed, or that party divisions would disappear."

Senator Susan Collins, a Republican from Maine, says she finds, "with all due deference to our male colleagues, that women's styles tend to be more collaborative." Kelly Dittmar, a scholar at the Center for American Women and Politics and a political science professor at Rutgers University says, "Women just want to get things done. They're not in it for the show."

Politics and government are complex issues and offer very few straight-line answers, but surveys and reports from other areas of the world also point to greater collaboration amongst women across party lines. It is very much worth noting also, that the data show that women in government everywhere pay greater attention to quality-of-life issues, those that directly impact the lives of individuals, such as health, education, leisure and social interactions, and the overall experience of life, measuring those things that the OECD refers to as 'subjective wellbeing'.

The OECD, the Organisation for Economic Cooperation and Development, is an international organisation that works with governments, policy makers and citizens, to shape policies that "foster prosperity, equality, opportunity and well-being for all." The OECD says that being able to measure people's quality of life is fundamental when assessing the progress of societies, and there is now widespread acknowledgement that measuring subjective wellbeing is an essential part of this assessment.

The organisation has produced guidelines for the collection and use of measures for this 'subjective well-being' which investigate people's lives and their feelings about issues such as income, jobs, housing, health, work and life-balance, education, social connections, civic engagement and governance, environment and personal security. Subjective wellbeing is, fundamentally, self-reported levels of satisfaction in people's quality of life.

Experts agree that quality of life increases across communities when women are active in positions of leadership in government. Social science researchers Shannon Bell and Richard York report in their 2014 paper *Life Satisfaction Across Nations: The Effects of Women's Political Status and Public Priorities,* that "people report the highest levels of life satisfaction in nations where women have greater political representation, where military spending is low, and where health care spending is high, controlling for a variety of other factors. GDP per capita, urbanization, and natural resource exploitation are not clearly associated with life satisfaction.

These findings suggest that nations may be able to improve the subjective quality of life of people without increasing material wealth or natural resource consumption, by increasing gender equality in politics, and reorganising public spending priorities, which latter, has been seen to occur, anyway, when women are active in political and government policy- and decision-making.

A previously cited 2019 ILO report based on an analysis of data from 186 countries, for the period 1991-2017, found that an increase in female employment is positively associated with GDP growth.

The World Economic Forum's 2014 Global Gender Gap Report found a positive correlation between gender equality and per capita GDP. GDP measures the size of a country's economy, is influenced by a country's monetary policy and is, therefore, in many ways a reflection of the quality of a country's government.

One of the primary factors on which a country's economy and, therefore, its GDP depends is human capital. Denying women's right to contribute to a country's economy is choosing to curtail the value of a country's GDP and depriving the country of wealth, by depriving the country of the maximum available human capital.

Given what we know of women's capabilities and of women's accomplishments despite the restrictions under which they have been forced to function across all these millennia, it would be very difficult to overstate the need for transformation in our families and societies. Harvard Business Review writes that with regard to the events of 2020 – the pandemic, the global demonstrations of frustration with racism and sexism, and of dissatisfaction with policing and such – leaders of the worlds of both business and politics have been facing a real-time leadership test…a huge crisis, unlike anything seen in our lifetimes, [that] renders experience and expertise irrelevant. Whatever the future brings, one thing is certain, think the writers at HBR, those in charge will be judged on how they manage this crisis — and nowhere are the stakes higher than in government.

Further, Harvard Business Review continues, "The best way to evaluate leaders' performance, has always been to look at how their teams and followers are performing, especially compared to others…In this competition, few comments have received more attention than the stellar performance of female leaders."

The growing body of evidence around women in government demonstrates, beyond the shadow of a doubt, that when women are allowed to exercise the right to participate in the government of countries and communities, conditions improve. There is no longer any real question in that regard. At every level, from the village council to the houses of parliament, from the federal government to regional bodies and global organizations, whenever and wherever women are allowed to fully exercise the right to participate and contribute, the legislative and administrative focus always begins to shift and widen to address the issues that improve the everyday lives of the community. Matters of important and always urgent concern, such as health, education, small business, the environment, peace and safety, minimum wage and public transportation, migration, child care, sanitation, food supply, to name just a few, generally experience increased engagement when women are active in the legislative and policy making rooms.

The inclusion of women in political and governmental decision-making provides a balance that more accurately reflects the composition of society. Inclusion enhances the legitimacy of political and administrative processes; it makes them more democratic and responsive to the concerns and perspectives of all segments of society. History and data show that sectors such as civil liberties, human development indices, electoral process and pluralism decline or fail to improve when women are excluded from political participation.

The history of countries – and focused research findings – have established overwhelmingly, that areas such as labour participation, functioning of government, elections, political culture and overall political participation are positively affected when women are allowed political participation. In fact, women are written deeply into the political history of many countries, whether it is acknowledged or not. Women have always been foot soldiers and worker bees in political movements – labour, freedom and independence, environmental protection and more – able to reach sectors and communities which men could not, bringing a perspective not available to men, and engaging strategies and communication not instinctive or familiar to men.

Entry into the spheres of government, and that is to say politics, continues to be a dangerous move for women everywhere, in any of a number of ways, and that has to be addressed. Women who choose to enter this arena are excoriated personally, have their names routinely dragged through the mud with lies, fabrication and malicious misrepresentation. Women are threatened with and subjected to physical violence that sometimes extends to rape and murder, and often with impunity. With this, as with so many other matters, however, the only way out is through. It is necessary that many more women engage in the politics and government of countries in order that there come equality and change in government and other areas, and in order that political leadership becomes safer for women, by becoming routine, normal and accepted as a natural occurrence, as just a matter of fact.

Political office is often a thankless and unreliable job, and it is many times so for women, specifically because of the unique nature of the risks to which women are exposed when they choose this path of service. But everywhere, change for the betterment of communities and the lives of individuals in society, occurs in direct proportion to the increase in the numbers of women in government and decision making. That is now beyond doubt, but the numbers and proportions of women in office are still insufficient to resist overwhelm; the numbers must be made to rise.

Government is just another example of the occasions and areas where there truly is strength in numbers and where diversity is undoubtedly the greatest strength. There must be more women leaders in the offices, Houses and hallways of government, at every level. It is helpful to all segments of society. Immeasurable and lasting good will comes from it. The evidence, mounting by the second, supports this.

MANY WOMEN IN LEADERSHIP
=
A BETTER WORLD

Finally I was able to see that if I had a contribution I wanted to make, I must do it, despite what others said.
- Wangari Maathai

As the old cigarette commercial aimed at women used to go, "We've come a long, baby." And, as everyone is very much aware, there is a long way still to go. A very long way! The advance must not be stopped. Progress must not be halted. Women must keep pressing forward. There can no stopping now. The viability of the very planet is at stake, and with it the survival and wellbeing of the human race and the creatures that sustain, enhance and ennoble human living.

Human civilisation has arrived at a critical moment in its development. If the global society is to come through alive and well, i.e. capable of continuing to make progress, it is vital that the capacities, the skills, the contributions of women be embraced. For far too long, women have been denied expression, and human societies deprived of great benefit. That state of deprivation is a big part of what created this now clearly-untenable situation in the first place. Women and communities must ensure that the movement for women's leadership contribution continues to forge ahead so that human living be elevated.

Leadership opportunities are everywhere. They exist in homes, families and communities. They are prevalent in play-space and workplace, in every sector of human living – in politics, business, academia, the arts, sports, religions, in leisure and entertainment – literally everywhere. These opportunities should be available to women, by right, as to men. They, clearly, are not going to be handed to women. It is women, themselves, who must go get them, claim them, inhabit them. Leadership positions will not ever be happily – or even, politely – handed over to women. It never is the case that a group cede power willingly. There is no evidence to suggest that it will occur in this case. Indeed, the history has been clear, and the bulk of available evidence very clearly indicates that unless women fight for it, and demand it and not rest until they achieve it, it never will. Fighting is a dangerous activity. It is sometimes deadly.

On November 30th, 2018, the Honduran National Criminal Court convicted seven men of the murder of human rights defender Berta Caceres. The Court found that the men had been hired by executives within Desa, a company constructing a dam in indigenous Lenca territory, to carry out her killing on March 3rd, 2016. Desarrollos Energéticos SA (Desa), is the Honduran company which was building the Agua Zarca dam, a project which Berta and COPINH (Frontline Defenders) had strongly opposed and campaigned against.

In March, 2020, Erin Templeton expressed her disappointment with US presidential politics in an article in the Guardian's International Edition entitled *Elizabeth Warren was the ideal candidate, but there was only one problem...she was a woman.* "In the US," she wrote, "it still seems that a smart, well-qualified hopeful must always lose to an ageing white man." She meant a smart, well-qualified woman.

In August 2018, African Feminism tweeted, "Diane Rwigara still remains in custody. Her only crime - her bid for the Rwandan Presidency." That same month, Lord Abraham Mutai also tweeted 2010, "Victoria Ingabure wanted to run for Presidency of Rwanda as sole opposition candidate to DICTATOR @PaulKagame, she was arrested, jailed for 15 yrs. 2017, Diane Rwigara wanted to run for Presidency, arrested, now facing 20 yrs. Rise up WOMEN."

In October, 2019, The Japan Times had this to say in an article entitled, *Japan's labor market is still rigged against women* – "Despite improving gender equality in the raw employment numbers, Japan is still struggling with equality in the workplace. Despite declaring that 30 percent of management positions would be held by women by 2020, the government of Prime Minister Shinzo Abe has had to content itself with only 13 percent. That is probably holding down both productivity — because women's talents are being wasted — and the fertility rate, thus compounding the country's long-term economic challenges."

In Brazil, two policemen were arrested in 2019 and charged with the assassination of Rio de Janeiro activist and city councillor, Marielle Franco. Investigations indicate that she was executed by a group known as "The Crime Bureau", an organisation which, writes David Miranda, "commits murder at the bidding of politicians, criminals, right-wing paramilitary "militias", and whoever else has a few hundred thousand reais to pay for the murder of someone they don't like. "This time," he goes on to say, "they killed a noble woman who stood up for the best of causes – an activist who put her life and political power at the service of those who have been historically oppressed in a society beset by profound inequality."

In 2018, the Pew Research Center published a finding that "For women working in science, technology, engineering or math (STEM) jobs, the workplace is a different, sometimes more hostile environment than the one their male co-workers experience. Discrimination and sexual harassment are seen as more frequent, and gender is perceived as more of an impediment than an advantage to career success."

At a 2020 ceremony to recognize the landmark Fourth World Conference on Women, held in Beijing in 1995, United Nations Secretary-General António Guterres told a high-level General Assembly meeting that it must review progress. "It starts with the equal representation of women in leadership positions – in Governments, boardrooms, in climate negotiations and at the peace table – everywhere decisions are taken that affect people's lives," he said. "This is fundamentally a question of power."

He is correct. It is a question of power. Power that has been the stronghold of men for millennia and that men are very clearly not particularly eager to share. Studies, surveys and research of various kinds conducted in many parts of the world provide real, incontrovertible and mathematical data, as well as ample qualitative evidence proving that gender equality and the inclusion of women in the structures of power and leadership are of benefit to all – men very much included; men just as much as any. Yet women continue to struggle for opportunities to participate fully. In much of the world today, women are generally being seen to be "more present" – because women are standing up, protesting, supporting each other, shining a light for each other – but nowhere are women on an equal footing with men.

All around the word, women's gifts, talents and abilities are being made to go to waste.

When she was the head of UNWomen, Michelle Bachelet, two-time President of Chile and currently United Nations High Commissioner for Human Rights, made a point of highlighting her belief that, "Women's strength, women's industry, women's wisdom are humankind's greatest untapped resource...Gender equality must become a lived reality...We simply can no longer afford to deny the full potential of one half of the population."

As if the world actually needed such corroboration, Entrepreneur magazine tells us that according to the International Federation of Business and Professional Women, women do have the chops to become transformational leaders. As Winnie Byanyima and Bachelet herself have specified, however, the changes occur when women are present in sufficient numbers. Numbers make all the difference. "There is strength in numbers" is both cliché and truth.

Critical mass is a concept borrowed from nuclear physics. It refers to the smallest amount of fissile material needed for a sustained nuclear chain reaction. In general terms, it describes an irreversible change, a launch that cannot be stopped, into a new situation or process. The UN believes that the figure of 30% forms the 'critical mass' necessary for women to make a visible impact on the style and content of the political decision-making process. "In its historical context," writes Drude Dahlerup, "the critical mass argument should be interpreted as an attempt to shift the focus from women's alleged lack of qualifications in politics to a critique of the conditions women meet when entering the political arena in small numbers. It points to the inequality embedded in the political norms and culture, which in most countries developed before women had access to the political arena."

Of course, whether 30% is the magic number is debatable. Indeed, given that we are dealing with human beings, any figure would be, but the idea of a tipping-point is reasonable and applicable to every area of human living, and it would not be much of a stretch at all, to imagine that a 50/50 split would likely be that point, and would actually be the ideal balance, in this particular case. The idea of the "token" woman, aside, the history of every sector and sheer mathematics – not to mention politics itself – very clearly demonstrates that women do get overrun – that women's ability to be effective is challenged even when they are in the majority – Rwanda being an example. When the numbers are low the potential effectiveness is systematically obstructed, and often completely negated.

In every part of the world, there are women leading the work to make the world a better, safer, healthier, more equal place for everyone. They are doing this through above and below the radar, out loud and underground, through social and political activism and art, through education – formal, informal and non-formal, on the interwebs and on the streets; on beaches and riverbanks, steppes, prairies and mountain slopes; in homes, coffeeshops and universities, in high-rise buildings and grass huts. Women are travelling by boat, bicycle and foot, where necessary.

Women are inching towards boundaries and restraining lines, and are pushing hard against the limitations and restrictions, so progress is being made. Every day women are cracking class ceilings and breaking down barriers. In many places of the world, men are joining forces with women to support the equality of women across all sectors of society. While progress does not always come in leaps and bounds, women are taking steps and every step that any woman takes, no matter how small it might seem, brings all women closer to a state of equality. Every step, no matter how small, opens up yet another door into a better world for everyone. Women-in-leadership gets to become the norm. The world shall get to critical mass, to paradigm shift, to CHANGE. Women leaders are already on the job. More women leaders are on their way.

It is a movement that cannot be stopped; will not be stopped. It is a movement for protection and preservation, of the peoples of the earth and of the earth itself and, eventually, enough people will come on board and critical mass will have been achieved, and the world will be a different and better, more equitable and hopefully, safer place.

For those who wish to poke holes in the "women are better leaders" arguments, the firstrate Harvard Business Review offers a menu of legitimate qualifiers that include this statement: *One of the paradoxical consequences of sexism is that it elevates the quality of female leaders. Because women need to work harder to persuade others that they have the leadership talent it takes, they end up being more qualified and more talented when they are selected for leadership roles.*

The idea that women do not work as hard as men or that women are somehow not capable of working as hard as men, and that this therefore disqualifies them for leadership is nonsense. It has been disproved time and time again. The old clichés about women's work being never done or about women's second shift, came into being precisely because women have always had to juggle roles and responsibilities in ways that men have not, to an extent that men fail to comprehend – and the having had to live these lives does confer a valuable qualification upon women. Even Margaret Thatcher was able to grasp the logic. "The many management qualities needed to make a home, give women an ability to deal with a variety of problems so quickly. And it's that versatility and decisiveness which is so valuable in public life," she once said.

Over and over again, women have been forced to prove that they are capable workers and leaders, and contributors of equal value to communities. That should never have been necessary, but it was and women have proved themselves. Women have passed every test.

Women know that being in leadership means owning one's skills and ambitions and supporting those of others. It means being systematic about acknowledging innate abilities and talents and developing the necessary skill in using them. It means being informed and aware, and sharing information and opportunity. Being in leadership means acknowledging the work that other women have already done and stepping up to add to it. It means knowing that the possibilities exist and are endless, and that each is worth pursuing – those that exist on the small scale as much as those in the largest arenas. A good leader is also firm, compassionate, brave and judicious, and women are each of these things. Women possess all of these characteristics and qualities and are capable of accomplishing any feat of leadership that men can.

Women have a right, no less right than do men, to experience, exercise and express their leadership capabilities, for the benefit of themselves, their families and communities, without these impediments. There is still much to be done and a long way to go, and it is women who must do what needs to be done. Men will not do it. States will not do it. Religions will not do it. Institutions and systems will not do it. They will continue to resist and pushback as they have all done at some point, and they will come on board eventually, one by one, perhaps as slowly yet as they have so far, but come they will, as long as women keep on pushing, prodding, demanding, investing. It's a long game. There will be no overnight change of heart.

Women must continue to influence and build institutions and businesses, and must create their very own positions of leadership – and propagate the new, revised rules. Women must ask less timidly – unapologetically! – for what they want, and compete more boldly and vigorously to achieve and acquire them. Women will come to inhabit and function in leadership roles as easily, comfortably and naturally as do men, but must not necessarily seek to do so in the ways that men have. It is imperative and indeed, best overall, that women "be themselves" and so, be the change that the leadership structures so truly – and sorely – need.

So, of necessity, women must also continue to seek ways to strip away generations – centuries! – of conditioning into inferiority and self-doubt, and reorder lives and renegotiate relationships to activate and sustain this new reality.

As women continue to create, accept and relentlessly keep going after opportunities to exercise leadership, men will see the light – the benefits! – and become allies and supporters. They will find that the transformation that comes is absolutely beneficial to them. Men must be encouraged to understand this. The world that women want is one in which there is partnership – equal partnership – with equal access, opportunity and possibility for contribution and leadership at all levels in every sector, and men must come to know that it will serve the highest interests of men, also. Men must come to know that, with women's progress comes, also, women's enhanced ability to support them!

Women's relationships with other women are critical considerations always. They are of equal import in the movement for equality generally, and especially in the realms of leadership. Simmons College, now Simmons University, was instituted in Massachusetts in the United States on an endowment from John Simmons, a man who earned his wealth in the clothing manufacturing business in Boston in the middle of the 19th century. When Simmons died in 1870, his will provided for his surviving family – two daughters and two granddaughters – as well as for the founding of an educational institution, it says on the university's website.

His instructions were, "It is my will to found and endow an institution to be called Simmons Female College, for the purpose of teaching medicine, music, drawing, designing, telegraphy, and other branches of art, science, and industry best calculated to enable the scholars to acquire an independent livelihood."

Simmons College once declared itself an institution "with a deeply-cherished history of visionary thinking, social responsibility, and commitment to the advancement and empowerment of women." The latest iteration of that vision says that Simmons University will be seen as "the global expert in educating women for their own empowerment and for leadership." Simmons strongly encourages its alumnae to support and mentor one another, and commit to helping each other make their way successfully through the world as created by men, improving it as they do so, and clearing the way for more women to achieve success and leadership in their chosen fields.

Men have long enjoyed the benefits of clubs, fraternities, lodges and guilds that excluded women, and this was not only because women were not men. Often the members of these associations were men with skills or beliefs in common who swore to love, protect, serve, fight for and be faithful to each other and the brotherhood for life, men operating tight networks of social and commercial business.

Writing in Psychology Today, Dr. Audrey Nelson recalls, "Growing up, I remember that my father, who was an accountant, was a member of the Optimist Club. I also remember that the membership was all white males, no women or other races. When my father purchased the family car, he went to a member of the Optimist Club who owned a car dealership. When he needed car insurance, he went to a member of the Optimist Club."

Katie Derham is a British newscaster and presenter, and member of Sorority, a private club which describes itself as "a trusted circle of international businesswomen, entrepreneurs, leaders and pioneers". She is quoted on the organisation's website as saying, "Women are very good at being part of a gang, being collegiate, but we don't have much structure to be collegiate. The Sorority is creating something which is both very pleasurable and professionally useful as well."

"Women are a long way from reaching parity with men in the executive suites and boardrooms of Fortune 500 companies," Nelson also says, "But...we now know some of the tricks men have used to get to the top. One of the well-known tricks of the trade is "It's who you know." That can make it or break it in the business world. No one gets to the top alone. And women cannot do it without networking with men and seeking men as mentors. Male mentors can help women understand the critical world of how men do business, and how to talk so men will listen and help them make it to the top. Women need both male and female mentors. Having both will ensure that she learns the tricks of the trade."

It is well that women are being more intentional and specific about their associations and about creating networks that provide dedicated support and sisterhood that they can rely on in the climb. Indeed, it is necessary that they do so to even greater degree. As Nelson says, no one can get to the top all by herself. Women need the support of other women and women must be instinctive about providing this support. The long game of equality and leadership demands it.

"We need to reverse the stereotype that women don't support other women," says Shelley Zalis of ForbesWoman, and also, "I always say a woman alone has power; collectively we have impact. Traditionally we have been taught to be competitive with one another, because there was such a scarcity of jobs at the top. It's so clear that strategy doesn't work. The truth is that raising each other up and channelling the power of collaboration is truly how we'll change the equation— and have a lot more fun along the way."

And that fun, and the journey itself, will be all the more remarkable if also women keep firmly in mind that leadership is exercised across each and every domain and on every level of those realms; that leadership is fluid. In other words, it would serve women to be always conscious that in every role any woman plays, whatever her station in life, there is opportunity for leadership and she should be supported. Every single instance of a woman exercising her

capacity for leadership is another drop in the bucket –
whether she does so as the CEO making a significant
decision in a professional setting, or she is a woman
restricted by social or religious traditions who manages
one act of leadership in her home that plants the seed in
the consciousness of a child. Both are important. Both
are indispensable.

That equation of which Zalis speaks must be
balanced, not merely changed. It is not an equation
otherwise and what the world needs most, what women
are working towards is a situation in which the values
of the two expressions – women and men – are equal.
They must be held to be so, shown to be so, and
maintained that way – of equal value.

It has already been proven on myriad occasions that
it would serve the world best. The evidence already
exists, is clearly in evidence. The journey to a world in
which there are many women in leadership, enough
women leaders to shift the proverbial paradigm, has
been in progress for centuries. All over the world and
throughout all the ages, women have been stepping up,
gearing up, preparing themselves and their children.
Now they are walking into the arenas, offices, piazzas,
Houses, roadways and elevators in ever greater
numbers. They have already moved the world closer to
an era of equality, mutual support and reciprocal
upholding.

There will come that time when the abilities and
capacities of women are accepted and, indeed,
welcomed all across every sector of human living,

effortlessly, instinctively, naturally and we will have stepped into that era.

There will come that time when there will be so many women comfortably and successfully inhabiting positions of leadership in our communities and societies that it will be impossible to imagine life being any other way.

It is a sisterhood of women who will lead the world into that time, a sisterhood of many women.

WORD

There is so very much going on in our world, as I write this! Everywhere, people still are dying of a brand-new disease that, until it actually hit us, we knew nothing about.

On large continents and small islands around the world, people are protesting loudly and in large groups about the failures of systems, the inefficiencies of bureaucracy, against the deaths of individuals, the destruction of families and the deterioration of communities, brought about by institutionalised racism, state-sanctioned violence and historical inequities combined now, with a global health hazard wreaking nothing but havoc.

The general population of the planet is experiencing financial distress, social upheaval and cultural disruption, added to the already ongoing wars, institutionalised injustice and intractable poverty. Everywhere, people are asking, "Can we get out of here?" "How do we set things right again?" "How do we come back from this?" "Can we move forward from here?"

The answers are provisional at best. "The jury is out on whether humanity will emerge stronger and better equipped to work together, or if distrust and isolation will increase," writes Calene Malik.

"To build back better, we cannot leave the voices of women and youth behind," said Maria Fernanda Espinosa Garces, president of the UN General Assembly 2018-2019, speaking at the World Government Summit. "We need to craft a world that is more sustainable and more resilient, free from inequalities and injustice. It is clear that women are agents of transformation, of building back better a world for all."

Some, however, are hopeful and optimistic. The tiny seed of trust in human resilience is still alive in many people. The race will survive. It is being depleted, but it shall not be defeated.

There is, obviously, very much work to be done to set the world to rights, even just to give a moment of reprieve and respite! This demands everybody and our cats chipping in, scrubbing in, falling in, leaning in, digging through, to pull us away from this yawning hole. Any lesser effort, and we fall in. All of us.

This is an important time. It is an inflection point that could bring us to reconciliation and ascending, on a scale beyond our wildest dreams. It could be the portal into a brand-new world of communication and connection buttressed by goodwill and rightness. It could lead us into a world far better than the one we have lost.

I am hopeful. My faith in the power and resilience of the human spirit wanes at least as often as it waxes, but it never altogether fails. My faith in the power of women to be the difference never wanes. Like the TEDWomen people, I believe unshakably, in the power of women to affect lives, heal communities and change the world. I know that women have the capacity and the ability to improve the world and I believe beyond the shadow of a doubt that women have the right to participate and contribute this ability to the fullest extent that we desire. I know that when women do well, when women are fully engaged and included, everyone benefits, everybody does better.

I believe that is where real leadership lies. I believe that is what the world needs now. This is what the people of the world will need deep into the foreseeable future and beyond. This is what women bring. So, yeah, nah! Not *any* woman. Not *more* women. M*any* women.

Many women in leadership will absolutely, without question, bring us a better world. I know that. I continue to work for that. You should, too. Many women in leadership will be a boon to all of us.

Another world is not only possible, she is on her way.

On a quiet day, I can hear her breathing.

-    Arundhati Roy

WHEN WOMEN LEAD

235

ABOUT THE AUTHOR

Shirley Osborne is a writer, a politician and a women's leadership advocate.

For more than twenty-five years, Osborne has served organisations, women and girls, and governments in several roles, all of them either focused on the empowerment and advancement of women or that placed her in a position from which she could support women in positions of leadership and women aspiring to leadership.

She is the founder of the Girls' Education Project and one of the co-founders of the Arizona Girls' Roundtable. She has been a leadership facilitator for the World Academy for the Future of Women at SIAS University in China.

Osborne has an MBA from Simmons University in Boston, Massachusetts, USA, an institution with a deeply-cherished history of visionary thinking, social responsibility, and commitment to the advancement and empowerment of women, the vision statement of which says it will be seen as "the global expert in educating women for their own empowerment and for leadership."

MANY WOMEN IN LEADERSHIP

=

A BETTER WORLD

In this book, the single premise is that when women lead, all kinds of good things happen and get done that would not have happened or been done otherwise, because they could not come about unless women were involved.

And it must be glaringly obvious to everyone that the world – our world – this world that is inhabited by both women and men, is desperately in need of having many more good things happen.

This book highlights some of women's contributions and many of the reasons why women must step up boldly, confidently and unapologetically, and inhabit the ranks of leadership.